The Long Walk Home:
A Veteran's Barefoot Journey Across America

Second Edition

by

Ron Zaleski

All profits go directly to
TheLongWalkHome.org

kamel press

All profits from the sale of this book go directly to
The Long Walk Home, a 501(c)3 non-profit
dedicated to helping Veterans make the transition
from military to civilian life.

Join us at
www.TheLongWalkHome.org
to see how you can help make a difference.

Proudly prepared for publication by Kamel Press, LLC - Belle Opelika, AL
ISBN-13:
     978-1-62487-111-5 – Paperback
     978-1-62487-113-9 – eBook

Library of Congress Control Number: 2023945217

Published in the USA.

DEDICATION

This book is dedicated to soldiers who left the war zone but brought the baggage of the battle back, only to succumb—the more than 22 Prisoners of War imprisoned in an internal war, believing death to be the only escape, who are murdered every day by their own hands on our own soil. They go mostly unnoticed, as do their families whose time in the impact zone of post-traumatic stress disorder (PTSD), traumatic brain injury (TBI), and moral injury is somehow considered acceptable collateral damage.

CONTENTS

DEDICATION 3

HOW TO READ THIS BOOK 1

INTRODUCTION 3

POOLSIDE: MY EPHIPHANY 4

THE APPALANCHIAN TRAIL: WALK ONE 8

A BEAR, AN ANGEL, AND GOD 10

TRAIL ANGEL 11

TRAIL INTERRUPTED 12

THREE SOLUTIONS 14

THE APPALACHIAN TRAIL: WALK TWO 18

MONSON 21

POLITICAL ALTERCATION 22

HYPOTHEMIA 24

THE RIGHT CATHOLIC 26

MIKE 27

IT DIDN'T AFFECT ME 28

UNCONVENTIONAL 20-YEAR-OLD 29

DAD'S WAR 30

TRAIL TRIVIA 31

VET'S ON THE TRAIL 34

POST-DISCHARGE: YEAR ONE 35

MOUNT AVERY 37

RECON MARINE 38

TONY 39

MARINE TRAINING 41

PARADISE 45

MOUNT WASHINGTON 49

THE BRAWL 50

DEPLETED URANIUM 54

DO MY FEET HURT? 56

COMBAT HAS NO EFFECT 57

AA AND ACOA 58

THE LUCKY B&B 59

THIRSTY JOE 61

INTEL 62

CAPTAIN MIKE 63

SERIAL KILLER 66

WASHINGTON, DC 67

THUNDER AND LIGHTING 70

EXTENDED ZERO DAYS 71

BACK ON THE TRAIL 72

TRAIL LORE 73

FOOD FOR THOUGHT 74

THE ROAD TO DAMASCUS 75

FLASHBACK 76

JAPANESE DOCUMENTARY 79

THE RAIN 80

GIARDIA 81

THE BOMB 82

MEDIA EVENT 84

THE KEYS 85

VALERIA 87

FIRST STEPS ACROSS AMERICA: JUNE 1, 2010 88

VETERAN SUICIDE 90

WHO CARES 91

A PLOT OF GRASS 92

THE ZOMBIE 93

A MOTHER'S LITANY 95

AMERICAN LEGION 96

LOST 97

ANGRY YOUNG VETS 98

VIETNAM 101

THE BROOKLYN BRIDGE 103

A CRY FOR HELP 105

MISSING WALLET 106

CHARACTER 107

ARE YOU RIGHT WITH THE LORD? 108

DIVORCE 109

MARRIAGE NUMBER ONE 110

DIVORCE NUMBER ONE 113

LIFE SPRING 114

MARRIAGE NUMBER TWO 116

WALKING ON COALS: SHANKSVILLE, PA 117

KICKED TO THE CURB 118

7 - DAY ADVENTIST 120

THE CAT 122

STAY OFF THE ROAD 123

REFORM SCHOOL 124

FAMILY 126

FACE OFF 129

CONQUERING MY NEGATIVE THOUGHTS 130

FINDING MY OWN STRENGHT 131

SUICIDE FIRST AID 132

THE TREE OF FREEDOM 135

MOVE A MOUNTAIN 136

THE DOG 137

GARBAGE 138

MISSING JEWELS 140

BABCIA 141

THE VA HOPITAL 142

SORRY TO DISSAPOINT 143

MAILING LIST 144

MORAL INJURY 145

THE VET UNDER THE BRIDGE 146

HOMECOMING 147

CIVILIANS AND MILITARY 148

PERRY COUNTY 150

JOHN COUTURE 151

CONGRESSMAN ROE 152

A FATHER'S ANGER 153

BARBARA 155

COLLATERAL DAMAGE: FAITH 156

BUFFALO 157

THE COYOTE 159

NATIVE AMERICAN CEREMONY 160

NATIVE AMERICAN GRANDMOTHERS 161

AN ENDLESS TRAIL OF TEARS 162

REDEFINING WORDS 163

COURAGE 164

DIRTY 165

MOCCASINS 167

VETERAN STUDENTS 168
THUMBLEWEED 170
CUFFED 171
IRON HOG 173
THE SHARP CRACK 175
EATING WORMS 176
THE ANGEL 179
PROGRESS 180
SILENTLY KILLING YOURSELF 181
LOSING A SON 182
THE FINAL DAY: MARCH 19, 2011 183
THE PETITION 184
THE SHIFT 185
A HOMELESS SHELTER 187
BREATHWORK 189
REBIRTH 191
EVERYTHING HAS AN IMPACT 193
EVERYONE HAS AN IMPACT 195
THE THROWN ROCK 196
NOTHING TO FORGIVE 197
IT'S NOT TOO LATE 198
YOU ARE NOT ALONE 200
SUICIDE-SAFER COMMUNITIES 201
PROVIDING A SACRED SPACE 202
ACKNOWLEDGMENT 205
10 CHALLENGES TO SERVICE 206
MENTORSHIP REQUIREMENTS: 221
LEVELS OF MENTORSHIP: 221

HOW TO READ THIS BOOK

When the first edition of this book came out, I struggled with the idea of providing all Ten Challenges to readers because they seem to work a lot better when one goes through them with a Mentor. It also allows me to connect with individuals and ask them to become a Mentor, themselves.

But it's not about me.

After seeing the impact of this book on the lives of Veterans and their support family, we decided it would be best to provide the Ten Challenges, as a whole, but we also wanted to provide context. What does that mean?

As you are reading through the book, you'll see some callout boxes that say things like "This explains what inspired Challenge X."

That doesn't mean you should drop everything and go do Challenge X. It does, however, provide context for when you get to that particular Challenge. The Ten Challenges have all been provided toward the back of the book and are there for anyone to complete. I recommend you complete them in the order of one through ten, as we've experimented to develop a progression that seems to ensure the most impact and help for those participating.

For those reading this book, however, I'd like to provide one additional Challenge: don't stop. When you complete the Ten Challenges, join us at www.TheLongWalkHome.org and share your story! You can leave us feedback, work through the Ten Challenges again, or explore what it might take to become a Mentor.

There are many success stories about the impact of taking the Ten Challenges. But don't take my word for it ... here are a few examples.

We had a young man who went to our Facebook page (Military to Civilian Life) saying he was in a dark place and another Veteran who I had known from NY when I was in business 40 plus years ago, now a therapist would read the posts and noticing his response reached out to him(Chris) and talked to him for hours over the course of several days. Chris had been one of the first Veterans I had mentored to take the Challenges. When he was almost done I told him, you can become a Mentor if you want. He said, "I hope you don't mind, but I already mentored a buddy who was drinking a fifth a day and had a gun in his mouth. I gave him the First

Challenge: What are you grateful for? It took him 2 days to answer it, but when he did it changed his life." You see he believed he was a monster and was set out to destroy himself and when he found something to be grateful for there was a shift in his perception and it changed everything.

We did a lot of our Challenges in small groups on Zoom. One of the groups had a Vietnam (VN) Era Marine who had isolated himself from other people. When he shared about taking the Challenge about getting out of his comfort zone, you could literally see the change in his eyes and face when he said, "I realized they weren't out to get me, and I actually enjoy talking to people now."

Another VN Era Veteran took the Challenges and said later that he didn't realize he had any problems and his wife thanked us for the change in her husband by making me a batch of chocolate chip cookies, one of my favorite 'thank you's.'

We started doing camping trips and one-day hikes to administer the Challenges which I believe are more impactful because you get unplugged from your normal routine and its distractions. On one such trip, we had a single mother (Army Veteran) bring her two daughters and you could see a shift in how they communicated and smiles that weren't there before.

Two men in their 30s from the war in the sandbox joined us on a campout thinking it was a mud run but did it anyway and said they would bring their wives with them on our next trip, which occurred several months later.

These are just a few of the stories, but everyone who takes the Challenges is impacted, and the more effort you put into it the more you get out of it.

We also help Veterans with other issues, but before we do they must take the first four Challenges. This shows us whether they want to improve their life or just want a handout enabling them to continue down the same path.

We will work with you, not for you.

Join us in the mission.

INTRODUCTION

My name is Ronald Charles Joseph Zaleski. In 2006 and 2007, I walked 2,174 miles (more than eight million steps) of the Appalachian Trail (AT) to create awareness for PTSD and Veteran suicide, barefoot. It became a penance to forgive myself.

I believe a consequence of Veteran suicide is that very few want to discuss it because it calls for accountability. It burdens all those who were left behind with a sense of guilt, making them new members of the ever-growing silent majority.

In 2010 and 2011, after a few years of being impatient and feeling incomplete, I walked 3,400 miles barefoot across the United States of America to implement a solution. For ten and a half months, I carried a sign that read, "18 Veterans a day commit suicide," and collected signatures for a petition to provide mandatory counseling for all military personnel prior to discharge. Since 2011, the number has swelled to 22 and has only recently begun to decrease. As of this writing (2021), the estimate is again approximately 18; however, that fails to reflect Reservist/ Guardsmen or suicides that are unconfirmed.

My journey little more than a decade ago took me through heat waves, blizzards, the halls of Washington, DC, and, hardest of all, the lives of those who couldn't be consoled for the loss of someone to suicide. I realized the United States isn't defined by its government, but by its citizens. We all carry the responsibility to make positive changes in our country, our lives, and the lives of others. This is the story about my long walk home and how it transformed me; my hope is that it may benefit others who are on their own journey.

I have chosen to capitalize the words Veteran, Veterans, Vet, and Vets in honor of my fellow Veterans. I also capitalize Marine, Soldier, Service member, etc., although there are occasions I simply refer to 'soldiers' as a general description of all those who selflessly serve their nation.

POOLSIDE: MY EPHIPHANY

It was six o'clock on a summer morning in 2005 in Flanders, a small hamlet of South Hampton, New York. I was opening the gym, an 18,000 square foot facility that my family had constructed on three acres of waterfront property from a garage and chicken coop. We built racquetball courts, floating docks, an indoor heated pool, a hot tub, a sauna, a scuba shop, and a nail salon. We had two weight circuits, cardio machines, tanning beds, rowing teams, aerobic classes, martial arts, personal trainers, and a summer camp.

It was my sanctuary from the rest of the world, where I did as I pleased. That morning, as usual, I cleaned the bath-rooms, assessed the equipment, greeted the early rising members, sold a few drinks, and reviewed some paperwork (my least favorite task). I was minding my own business, as happy as if in my right mind.

I was looking forward to the afternoon because, after a few more hours of manning the counter, I would be instructing a bunch of five-year-olds how to swim (my favorite class). After they arrived and were herded into the changing rooms to slip into their bathing suits, we made our way to the pool. Walking on a floor that I had helped tile, warmed by the sun filtering through the roof of my greenhouse overlooking Flanders Bay, I felt right as rain, oblivious to what was about to happen.

On that short walk, one little boy asked, "How come you don't wear shoes?"

It was a question I was asked a lot over the years, to which my typical response was, "I don't feel like it, you got a problem with that?" But in that space between a question and a thought (where infinity is found), it was as if God were speaking to me through this boy, asking, "What are you doing?"

I stopped in my tracks, standing in my swimsuit, facing this collection of boundless energy and sponges of curiosity while they waited for my answer. In an instant outside of time, I started drowning in a whirlpool of emotions and memories. Feelings of anger, guilt, shame, hopelessness, doubt, indig-nation, grief, and confusion engulfed me in what seemed like a lifetime as I relived the past. Where had I been all those years?

Working on freighters halfway around the world. Winning the draft lottery (lucky number 34) and joining the Marines with orders to go to Vietnam (which were changed so I remained stateside). Becoming part of the acceptable collateral damage. Living in the woods. Going to college. Losing myself. Marrying. Having children. Collecting divorces. Fighting with the town and any other form of authority. Walking 300 miles of the Appalachian Trail (1998) in search of peace.

Now, after all those life experiences, I stood there having an epiphany: all those years, I'd been held hostage by my own anger, stopped from truly living life. I was my own victim.

Eight long pool-room seconds passed while 33 years flew by in my mind. Then I spoke. "I did it as a memorial for my friends that died and suffered while I was in the Marines." That was the first time since taking off my shoes in 1972 that I had ever told anybody why. Before that day, it was just an act of defiance—a hollow memorial—and a meaningless penance that did nothing for the ones I told myself it was to honor, including those that would continue to join the swelling ranks.

My quick sound bite seemed to satisfy the five-year-old's curiosity. He was a junior Darwin seeing an unknown animal, observing it from every angle, touching, prodding, and poking it. Then being told it has a name and dropping it to the ground, thinking it's not special anymore and there's nothing else to learn because the name explained it all, stripping away its mystery.

On the steps of the pool, their class was over in half an hour, but my discovery just led me to new questions. What am I going to do about it? Why didn't I speak before?

My new journey had just started, and life would never be the same.

People say, "When you're ready, the master shows up." I say, "When you're ready, you show up." I believe the master is always available, but I have caller ID and you only get me by accident.

Months after that pool-side moment, when caught off guard, I was driven to do something. In retrospect, my drive was probably precipitated by the constant televising surrounding 9/11 stirring up memories and feelings I'd suppressed about the Vietnam era.

I replayed nights of young men screaming in the barracks while they slept, the suicides, the military deaths on both sides, and the millions of unarmed civilian deaths caught in the middle. But mostly I replayed my guilt, shame, and anger.

I was hearing the same verbiage from our leaders that they used during the Vietnam era: "We have exhausted all attempts at resolving this conflict and our only recourse is war." My blood boiled; I couldn't believe it. Would they have spoken those words if it meant having their loved one on the front line?

If history repeated itself, there would be no comprehensive effort to correct the damage done to our warriors' spirit, the essence of who they were that dramatically changed after they were asked to do the unspeakable—and then told never speak about it.

Having buried my head in the sand of apathy for so many years, I was oblivious to the world around me. Doing a little research, I found that (due to the unending wars and international conflicts) 18 Veterans commit suicide each day.[1] That was just the tip of the iceberg. Laying beneath the surface were the homeless, incarcerated, drunks, addicts, dysfunctional families, spousal abuse, divorce, despair, victimization, and the insidious impact returning Soldiers would have on society as a whole as they affect all the people close to them.

I am not qualified to make judgments about going to war, not having all the information available, but I do believe Service members need help making the transition when they come home. We could help them prepare for their next mission: raising a family, being a healthy member of society, and becoming leaders of our country. Is the financial cost to ensure this happens deeply cutting into someone's bottom line, keeping us from making the morally correct decision to help those who serve in their healing? Or would such an effort threaten to end a flawed decision process by forcing us to relook at it and truly see all the damage war creates?

We are told war is human nature and will never end. We take young people that we taught their whole life—through family, religion, and society—not to kill, yet we force them to go against this belief by creating extreme prejudice in the military to kill. Then we put them in a life-or-death situation to help ensure they will actually kill another person. Do we make a sincere effort to get them back home, the way they left, or do we give up because we feel it's impossible and any attempt means admitting we're wrong? We're told we're protecting our country and way of life; is that truly the case or is that just another way of saying we will die (or send others to die) for a can of gas?

---

[1] According to The Military Times, Veteran suicide continues to be an issue. The number rose to roughly 22 Veteran suicides each day for the better part of a decade and only recently (2020) saw a decrease back to 18 suicides per day. According to America's Warrior Partnership, the actual number is upto 2.4 times the VA rate, equating to 44 deaths per day. Upon speaking with law enforcement officers, I learned those numbers are most likely low. Criteria for determining whether a death is a suicide varies by state. In an effort to protect families from the guilt associated with suicide, law enforcement will often document the death as an accident if the victim leaves no note

I began to wonder what would create the most awareness for this mission to provide all military personnel with the tools they need to integrate back into civilian life by addressing their emotional and moral wounds—not just their physical wounds. What came to mind was using the Appalachian Trail as a medium. If I walked the whole thing barefoot, surely that would get some attention for this cause and even make others aware of the opportunity such a walk affords to heal oneself.

That is where this journey begins.

———————◆•◆•◆———————

My new journey had just started,
and life would never be the same.

THE APPALANCHIAN TRAIL: WALK ONE

In 1998, two years after my first divorce, my ex-wife won custody of our two boys and took them to Colorado. I spoke to them daily while they lived in New York, but was unable to keep them in geographic proximity because I was that fool who was his own attorney. Before they left, agonizing about what to say to them, and not wanting to say anything that would cause them to feel guilty or unloved, I asked a friend for advice.

I rarely took guidance from anyone on anything, but was frantic and listened, repeating what she told me, "I love you and support you in whatever you want to do. If you're happy, then so am I. If you change your mind and want to come back, I will put you on the next flight out or come to get you." I was happy to see my sons' relief from the crushing weight of having to make me happy or equally heavy guilt for wanting to go, but it destroyed me.

I was distraught after they left. I gave power of attorney to Jessie, a trusted employee, to run the gym. "If I don't come back, sell the place and make sure my brother and father get the money I owe them." With that, I took off to walk the Appalachian Trail alone, hoping to get my head together because I knew, in my current state of mind, I would completely destroy what was left of my business.

Before leaving, I made a reservation to attend a "Conversations with God Retreat" at Black Oaks in North Carolina. I was desperate, having put God on a back burner because I couldn't understand why He allowed terrible things to happen. I planned to chat with Him while in the woods and either get some guidance or scream at Him.

On my way to the retreat, I felt I should stop at a church—slowly break myself in. I passed many, conjuring up excuses not to stop before I came to one out in the middle of nowhere that was closed. Telling myself for the tenth time that I should stop, I continued on. That was the last church I'd see before getting to my destination.

Out of nowhere, an acorn hit the windshield like a bullet. I looked up at the sky and saw nothing: no bird, no plane, no oak tree. There wasn't even a breeze—only open fields on either side. I turned the car around and went back to the closed church. I got out of my car and knelt at the locked door (my attempt at humility) and said the Lord's Prayer. I was unable to verbalize my feelings or do more than recite that simple prayer. It felt like God was watching and wanted to talk. He was giving me signs, but I struggled to read His writing.

I spent the weekend at the "Conversations with God" retreat. My perceptions at that time, including believing myself to be unforgivable and deserving of punishment (my interpretation of being a good Catholic), were challenged. The retreat was a jump start for my upcoming walk, allowing me to rethink my core beliefs.

It felt like God was watching and wanted to talk.

A BEAR, AN ANGEL, AND GOD

After the retreat, I visited my sister, Deb. Naturally, she asked, "Why are you doing this hike?"

I said, "I am going to talk to God, see my angel and a bear."

She simply said, "Okay," and dropped me off at Springer Mountain, the starting point of my hike. Looking back, maybe she was checking to see if I planned on cashing it in on the trail.

I had thought about wearing boots, as many people told me it wasn't possible to walk the Appalachian Trail barefoot, but I canned the idea for a few reasons.

First, having gone shoeless for so long, I figured it would likely have hurt more than going barefoot.

Second, nobody was going to tell me what I couldn't do.

Finally, what reason would I give people that knew me—to wear shoes now and not before.

It also helped that I didn't know where the boundaries of my limitations were.

Two weeks of walking later, on a mountain trail where roots hungrily clutched the dirt, I was heading north and reached a fork heading west when I heard the cry of a soul being ripped out. Laying down my pack to investigate its origin, a bear ran across the path 60 feet ahead of me towards the cry. *Great. Check bear off the list.* I put on my pack and continued north. The bear ran across again, in the opposite direction—this time 30 feet closer.

Then a cub, chasing after his mother, came up to my leg and walked with me like a puppy until we got to a tree. He climbed the trunk up to my eye level, looked at me, and cried. I looked at him, walked a little further down the path, and then sat down in wonder. If I took him, would his mother take him back or disown him because he had my smell? He didn't belong in my world and I couldn't take care of him in mine. Then it dawned on me: the cub symbolized my boys.

I cried, thanking God for this gift. "I don't need to see my angel or talk to you."

God, being God (perfect and all), gave me the other two requests anyway.

TRAIL ANGEL

A few days after the bear, I met hikers who talked of trail angels: people who give without expectation. It was a radical notion to me, giving anything without expecting something in return.

To me, it was just a myth.

One day, a hiker coming from the north told me there would be a trail angel at the base of the mountain I would come to the following day. The next morning, not wanting to miss him, I wrestled out of my sleeping bag under the cover of darkness and arrived at the south side of the mountain around 7 am. I waited for the trail angel for an hour before leaving.

Why would anyone set up in the middle of the woods anyway?

I continued on and hiked to the other side of the mountain. Where a dirt road intersected the trail, there he was with the back of his car open, giving out hot coffee, coco, soup, fruit, a birthday cake he had made for one of the female hikers, and other trail magic.

Stepping up to his vehicle, I grabbed food and ate like my life depended on it (which it kind of did). Within a short time, my mouth stuffed, feeling obligated and guilty, having only been concerned with getting all I could, I thought I should at least acknowledge him. "What's your trail name?"

"Rocket Man."

"When did you hike the trail?"

"Never."

"Never! Why do you do this?"

He said, "A man came and spoke at our church about trail angels and I thought, 'I can do that.' So, every week I make all this food for you and travel 32 miles one way."

I was shocked. "Why?"

"Because you're my heroes."

I got a lump in my throat and could hardly swallow what I had in my mouth. I choked out, "You're my hero. I could never see myself doing this."

Looking back, it's humorous to think that, every time I've said the word never, it wasn't never—like giving without expectation. I'm beginning to think that 'never' isn't supposed to be in my vocabulary.

I checked 'angel' off the list, even though I didn't see his wings.

TRAIL INTERRUPTED

After several hundred miles of walking, I decided to get off the trail. I had been walking for about three weeks and Jessie was stressed out and wanted me back. But first, I had to chat with God.

I went back into the woods and sat there waiting to hear from 'The Boss.' After three days of silence, I quietly asked, "God, what do you want me to do?"

What do you want to do?

I shook my head; it wasn't the answer I wanted. So I asked louder, getting the same answer, but louder. The third time I screamed and got the same answer screamed back at me. Embarrassedly I said, "Oh, I can do anything I want?"

To which I heard a relieved, Yes.

After returning home, reestablishing myself at the gym, and pouring myself into my work using what I had learned on my journey, my oldest son Zach came for a visit. We both participated in a process called 'radical honesty.' It was something I learned about from one of my fellow participants at the "Conversations with God" retreat. You tell your life story for two hours to another person, who then does the same, each finishing with what you admire and resent about the other person.

The woman I did it with at the retreat had only known me a few days. She was 5' 2" and 90 pounds and she took me to a remote beach for the process. She screamed how angry she was with me for being honest, then told me what she admired about me—she felt safe enough to do this with me.

When I asked my son to do it, he simply said, "You knew how I grew up."

"I know how I saw you grow up," I responded, "but not how you saw growing up."

He reluctantly agreed to give it a try. I spoke first, being totally exposed and vulnerable, which gave him permission to do likewise. When it was his turn, he was pretty tame at first, until he paused with a look of apprehension on his face and told me that he had attempted suicide twice after the divorce. He had been put in the middle and had to listen to us bad mouth one another, deliver messages, hand deliver money, spy, and be used as a pawn between two people he loved. On top of that, he felt somehow it was his fault that we divorced.

"If only I was better," he eventually added, "you two would still be married."

At that point, I went into shock. The world closed in around me as an unstoppable tide of anger rose. I mentally put the blame on my wife, the whole time trying to keep a poker face, but I knew it was my fault as well. My anger was at myself—that I had hurt someone I loved so much, but I was also grateful that he had failed in those two attempts.

Because of this process, our relationship became stronger. I had exposed my faults, weaknesses, and fears to him and allowed him to share what he thought of me. When we were done, we looked at each other with a new understanding. I was grateful he accepted me, and that he had turned out so well in spite of me.

I lived my life feeling I had learned so much about myself while on the walk. In the ensuing years, though, I ran through numerous relationships and was married and divorced a second time. After 9/11, I would eventually find that I carried much more baggage than I thought.

I lived my life feeling I had learned so much
about myself while on the walk.

THREE SOLUTIONS

During my experience on the Appalachian Trail (AT) in the late nineties, I met many people who had their act together and used the AT as a vehicle for their cause: battling cancer, saving the environment, educating others—making a difference. Those people were self-aware and focused, and I began to feel that other hikers might be a channel for me to get the word out. At this time, I wasn't politically connected or of any influence on a nationwide scale but I figured I could still make a difference, even if small.

In preparation for my second walk, I started telling people I planned to walk the entire AT barefoot to create awareness for Veteran PTSD and get legislation passed for mandatory counseling. Telling people before I went was a way for me to ensure I didn't change my mind and back out.

They would ask, "Why don't you just protest the war?"

I would answer, "I'll protest war the day we stop having divorce."

My thinking was simple: how can we stop war when people who say they love one another can't get along? I believe protesting war would just give it more power; people would be fueled to defend it. More importantly, my goal to help returning Veterans would be overshadowed.

When you know the truth about something, it doesn't need to be defended or judged—simply shared. I knew that Veterans needed and deserved more help than they were getting.

I got to know a member of my gym by teaching his son to swim. He liked my plan and invited me into his home to help formulate the most effective way to state my points. He was an artist who once ran for Senate (basically as a protest), then started to worry about what would happen if he actually won. His wife was a publicist for artists.

He was tall and lanky with a constant smile extending from his eyes, reminding me of the 1939 Jimmy Stewart "Mr. Smith Goes to Washington." His wife was a shorter version of warmth and hope, and his favorite aunt was his role model. In the '60s, at the age of 13, she rode her bike 10 miles to the Office for Civil Rights to help. She spent her whole life volunteering.

In turn, they were grooming their son to be an asset through the environment they raised him in: loving, clean, and void of any drama. At the end of the day, Adam Straus and his wife, Nicole, gave me an invaluable education on public relations and human nature during the time I got to know them better.

They taught me that most people can't retain more than three thoughts at a time and that the majority won't read anything that looks too long at first glance. Together, we came up with three solutions we felt would be the most beneficial to Veterans:

1. Grieving classes during boot camp to provide an understanding of the five stages (denial, anger, bargaining, depression, and acceptance) that surface when someone su ers a loss so that they can identify what they're feeling;

2. Mandatory counseling prior to discharge to strip away the stigma of asking for help (more so than the usual debriefing); and

3. Available support groups after transitioning to civilian life (thankfully, there are currently many available through the VA).

I intended to educate people along my journey and encourage them to write to their politicians. If active military personnel are acceptable collateral damage (a term I don't hear anymore—maybe it's too callous or politically incorrect) just because they comprise less than 3% of the population, then what about the 70% that live within that impact zone?

It is unacceptable.

Prior to walking the AT again, my parents came to Long Island from Florida for a visit. My relationship with my dad had been strained for years, but not simply because I was exactly like him.

When I arrived home from the Marines in 1972, he said, "I'm proud of you."

"I'm ashamed," I said, "I hate it. They call us baby killers. They spit on us; we were treated like heroes before we went in, then like criminals after we got out. What'd we really go over there for anyway?"

I could see he was shocked and disgusted, though silent. He turned his back on me and walked away. A wedge was created between us that never left.

Before my walk, we got together for lunch, which was just an excuse to do what was expected: say our goodbyes. We met at the local diner resembling an oversized RV that's been in the same spot for over 50 years. We sat facing each other in a booth with vintage Formica tables. My father and I wrapped up the small talk in the time between ordering our meal (which I couldn't tell you about if I wanted to) and getting it, while my mom sat in silence. I don't remember her saying much growing up. Sometimes it was as if she grew up with us under Dad's roof.

In that judgmental authoritative voice that puts me on automatic defense, he said, "Why in hell are you going on this trail! What are you torturing yourself for?"

I paused to control my gut reaction before responding, "When I was in the Marines, I had orders to Vietnam and, while home on leave, I prayed, 'God, I don't think I have the courage to not shoot another man. I'm afraid and want to live.' At the last minute, my orders were changed. I was grateful because I was prepared to go to prison for five years or face a firing squad for my conviction. The five others I was supposed to go with got shot, and two were killed, all while I remained stateside."

My father had a look of astonishment on his face.

I continued, "I felt guilt, shame, and anger. My decision not to wear shoes as a private memorial became a hollow memorial, a meaningless penance, an act of defiance helping no one. I can no longer live this way— my silence has allowed the problem to continue."

After a deafening moment of silence, an event 60 years in the past bubbled up from my father as he spoke under his breath, "When World War II ended, I rode home on a train and talked to the man sitting behind me that had spent five years in fox holes and trenches and said that he didn't know how to act when he got home. After a while, I turned back around to face the front and dozed off. The train hit a bump and a footlocker fell out of the overhead rack and hit him on the head, killing him instantly."

Dad slowly lowered his head and made a strange muffled sound; he was crying, for the second time in my life (the first time was when he thought he was going to lose me). "Why did God take him and not me? He spent the whole war in trenches. I was only there for five months."

He looked at me as if he'd just recognized me. "I'll do whatever I can to help."

Mom asked, "Is that why you never wore shoes?"

"That's why," I confirmed.

She sat there, staring into space with sorrow etched on her tired face, and said, almost as if to herself, "I don't even know my own son."

When we finished eating, I got up to leave when my father grabbed me, and he hugged me. I saw that look of pride in his eyes that I hadn't seen since 1972.

————◆•◆•◆————

When you know the truth about something,
it doesn't need to be defended
or judged—simply shared.

Planning what I set out to accomplish with walking the AT
inspired Challenge 2 Goals. That isn't saying that over the course
of my walks how I got there would change but the goal remained
the same; to prevent Veteran Suicide. In the back of the book all
the challenges are listed for you to take your own inward journey.

THE APPALACHIAN TRAIL: WALK TWO

My second ex-wife, with who I had remained friendly, agreed to get me to Mount Katahdin (5,268' elv.) on Memorial Day. It was a bit of irony—a holiday that began May 30th after the Civil War, celebrated by southern women to decorate soldiers' graves (both Union and Confederate), and yet it had since devolved into simply a day off for a barbecue for many, if not most. Before she dropped me off, we stopped at the closest diner to the approach trail in Millinocket.

The floor was well-sanded by the soles of shoes dragging grit, and one could see where flyers had been taken down years after the events were over had left un-faded spots on the wall. We were served by a middle-aged woman wearing a huge smile (part of her uniform) who asked why I wasn't wearing shoes. After I explained, she shared how her husband with 20 years of active duty in the Air Force was reactivated, sent to Iraq for 14 months, and had just arrived home a few days ago. She had prayed at the foot of her bed every evening and cried in the loneliness of the night for his safe return. That morning, she was one of the happiest people on the planet.

One of the patrons, a big burly guy, overheard the conversation and said, "Before her husband came home, she was a pain in the ass! We're happier than she is that he's home." He continued, "I could hug you for what you're doing."

So I got up, walked over, and hugged him. "Don't get any ideas," I joked, "I don't kiss on the first date." He turned beet red as his buddies laughed at him.

The first few days on the trail, I only saw a handful of people, but I did see millions of trees coating the landscape like green duckling down growing on the mountains. For days, I pushed through marshes where mosquitoes were so thick the air shimmered. Bitten countless times, I became nauseated discovering that sucking on raw garlic kept them (and people) away while I self-marinated for the bears. I heard that, when the settlers first came here, livestock would suffocate from mosquitoes blocking their airway. I felt safe, though, since my blood-sucking friends only caused a haze, not a total eclipse of the sun. The garlic was working. Mostly.

I was apprehensive of doing the entire trail barefoot, remembering the few hundred miles I did in 1998 when my feet learned to talk to me. That first hike taught me to adjust my pace, plan the number of hours to walk, and be mindful of placing my feet on the uneven surface. Meaning, if I didn't raise my foot enough, my toes would become polo mallets, smashing roots and rocks, reverberating up to my head. There were times I saw stars during the day. Once, walking through a marsh, sawgrass cut through my toe (guess that's why they call it sawgrass). I wrapped the toe in a napkin I'd saved to use for toilet paper and put tape over that to slow down the bleeding and keep it from snagging anything else.

The Jo-Mary reserve (600' to 2,235' elv. and 3.71 million acres) was owned by nearly 20 organizations: loggers, hunters, environmentalists, etc. It seemed like an odd combination—like pimps and ministers joining forces to reach wayward women. Walking through, I was greeted by a red pickup truck rattling on a dirt washboard of a road as Evert, the driver, stuck his head out the window and asked, "Where ya going?"

"To the entrance gate to meet my ride."

"You're going the wrong way."

Radioing the gate, he was told my ride was looking for me. "Hop in." I did. "What are you doing?" he asked.

I could hardly get the words out. "The suicides are my fault because I've done nothing." I started to cry.

When I looked at him, he was crying. He looked me in the eye and, gentle with affection, used his thumb to wipe a tear off my check, as one would do for a child. "I'm just like you. I've never been to war, but if it had been my buddies, or I saw the other horrors of war, I wouldn't be the same either."

After meeting my ride, we went to lunch at a diner that was famous among hikers for homemade coconut cream pie. The pies were made by the 80-year-old owner who had worked every day for over 50 years and had never traveled more than 27 miles from where she was born. It was hard for me to fathom why anyone, with all the mobility access we have in this day and age, would be such a homebody.

Entering through the screen door, we heard its single spring stretching to its limit just before slamming against the wooden frame. We sat down at a long table lined with chairs as a woman with two children and an older woman came in. One of the children, a little boy about five, was crying. When the mother leaned down and whispered in his ear, he stopped. After they sat down beside us, I played with the kid until our lunch came out.

I discovered that the pies weren't a myth; they were a legend. While we ate, I asked the mother why her son had been crying.

"My husband and I started a business canning soup. He's in the National Guard and was called in, given a week of training, and sent overseas for 13 months. Now my mother-in-law is helping me with the children while I run the business. He wants his dad."

After we finished eating, I played some more with the boy. A miniature version of Charlie Chaplin who just stopped, he looked me in the eyes and asked, "When is my dad coming home?" with the crisp force of an iceberg that crushed me speechless.

In that instant, I realized I was in way over my head and still learning what this walk was all about.

After we left, his eyes haunted me as thoughts. What am I doing? Does it matter? Is it enough? Somebody should do something.

Somebody should do something.

MONSON

I marched into Monson (900'elv.), a town of 687 people, carved out of the woods where the trees stand as sentinels at the edge of the 100-mile wilderness (which is actually just 87 miles, but who passes up a chance to stretch the truth?). My first stop was Lulu's Restaurant. I had my priorities and, at that moment, eating was at the top of the list. While there, I listened to the owner tell me about her husband who had recently come back from Iraq.

"Help me talk to him. He hasn't been the same since he got back last year. You know, the wives need a program too."

I sat quietly, listening as I ate, realizing there were so many unknown facets of this issue that needed to be addressed. My brother and I have a saying: 'it's easy when you don't know how.' For me, that translates that ignorance is bliss—until I become aware of something I want to change—and then find that my original ideas aren't enough. After finishing lunch and our conversation, I left the restaurant deep in thought.

My contemplations were eventually released, giving way to my next practical priority: laundry. I entered the nearby laundromat, where I wrapped myself in a towel someone had left and washed all my stuff: a tee-shirt, a regular shirt, underpants, shorts, and long pants. After dressing in clean clothes, I walked around the entire town (about a block and a half), running into locals who had already found out what I was doing. Each would tell me about Lulu's husband and how he needed help. He had left everyone he met with an impression of his anger and detachment.

On my way out of town the next day, I ran into him walking down the street, holding his little girl's hand. Seeing them together reminded me of a child holding a balloon; she was the only thing that kept him connected to this life. We talked about what I was doing and the war.

"It's all bullshit," he said, "The lies they tell you to get you in, and then the reality hits that it's not a John Wayne movie. It's all about money, not the freedom we fought for. And we're never free from what we've seen and done."

I had no answers for him, only another question for me. *What is freedom?*

That encounter teleported me back to an experience I had 33 years prior. I stood there motionless, letting time run through me. I recognized his anger.

POLITICAL ALTERCATION

Three decades earlier, after being home from the service a few years, I had taken over the family business (originally a scuba shop—expanded with a gym). I got a call from the town Building Department and was told they were going to shut me down because I hadn't gotten a Certificate of Occupancy (CO). I was livid.

"I lost my family and everything I own in a divorce except this and you're going to take that from me? Come on and do it—I'll burn the Town Hall down."

They hung up and, not much later, the police called saying they had a warrant for my arrest because I hadn't complied with the Building Department by getting my CO.

"Do I have to work while in jail?"

"No."

"Will you feed me?"

"Yes."

"Do I have to wear shoes?"

"No."

"Come and get me."

He laughed and hung up. They left me alone because I would have done it.

A few years later, after starting my transformation and calming down, I went to the Town Hall and stood before the Board to ask for forgiveness. I explained that, at the time of being noncompliant, I was under a lot of emotional stress because of the divorce and that I would like to get my CO and live in peace.

They all thanked me, except one woman who said, "When we tell you to jump, you ask 'how high?'." I didn't think much of it, being only one of the group, and was on my way.

A few days later, a notice to appear in court arrived. When I went, they told me to replace the curbing that was not in compliance or they would fine me and throw me in jail for the max. This went on every month for three years—new jumping orders, costing thousands of dollars each time. Evidently, they felt confident enough that I wasn't going to burn the Town Hall down to continue. My second wife didn't believe me when I told her of their persistence and its financial consequences. She finally accompanied me to court to see for herself.

When we left the judge's chambers, she cried, "I didn't believe you! It's worse than you said."

It finally ended when they had a change in leadership after the elections and I was given an apology (talk about consequences for your actions).

———◆•◆•◆———

"Come on and do it ...
I'll burn the Town Hall down."

HYPOTHEMIA

After my chance encounter with Lulu's husband, I left Monson behind, taking with me that visual of father and daughter holding hands—along with some pork chop bones from my earlier dinner to enjoy later. I came to a stream, swollen into a raging river from the rain and melting mountain snow. On the other side, I saw a man (his trail name was Lucky) and yelled, "How do I get across? Is there a shuttle or a Ford further up?"

"No," he called back, "you're on your own."

Three steps in, I was swept away by the current while Lucky ran off down the trail. (I found out later he had crossed further up where it was easier.) I was soaked to the bone. My cell phone, camera, matches, sweater, and pork chops were gone. Of all the things lost, I missed those pork chops the most. I looked forward to meeting that man on the other side of the stream to show my gratitude, but it never happened. Boy, he was Lucky.

It was still early after my soaking, so I repacked what little gear was left and continued walking. My pack, clothes, and the heat generated from walking kept me warm enough, though it started to rain, preventing me from drying out completely. The sun was setting and the temperature was dropping when I made it to the shelter (a three-sided palace with a roof, but no heat or plumbing) and, for the first time, became concerned about hypothermia.

I began to shiver like a pneumatic hammer and stiffen as my muscles started locking up. Fortunately, two other hikers were there and gave me a cup of hot tea. I took it in both hands, cupping it in my lap, hunching over it, gaining whatever heat I could like it was the only hot rock in a sweat lodge.

Sipping it, I could feel it warm my core on the way down my throat as I slowly rationed it, being careful not to waste any of its precious heat. I finally stopped shivering and wrapped myself in my wet homemade sleeping bag. I had been sitting on it to warm it up. It consisted of one thin felt blanket sewn inside Tyvek.

Out of context, a cup of tea may seem insignificant, but I believe it saved my life that night. When I ran into those same hikers later down the trail, they said they pitied me, which was fine by me—at that moment, I was without pride. Thanking them again, I knew I was unable to express the true extent of my gratitude.

Days and nights on the trail, void of human contact, blended into one another. The common thread of my days was being in a sea of green and the absence of manmade distractions, which had previously kept me unaware of myself. My time was spent engrossed in feelings of comfort and pain or deep in thought, making me occasionally oblivious to the wooden canopy I moved under. When I could see the sun's molten gold spread over the earth through the tapestry that hid me from the world, its warmth filled me—like a cat on a windowsill—with the light of life. Feeling safe at sunset, while the trees stood guard, I slept in the breathless bed of night.

During the day, I encountered people who told me their stories, or I heard myself tell them mine, triggering emotions I had buried. Feelings not yet fully processed would re-emerge as I revisited and examined them in this terrarium of silence. The only thing that broke my contemplation in these moments was my toes' unmindful attempt to dislodge rocks and roots connected to the earth's mantle; they quickly reminded me to be in the moment and pick up my feet.

———————◆•◆•◆———————

Out of context, a cup of tea may seem insignificant,
but I believe it saved my life that night.

Describing this incident falls short of the feeling of gratitude I had that day for a warm cup of tea and was also the inspiration for Challenge 1. In the back of the book all the challenges are listed for you to take your own inward journey.

THE RIGHT CATHOLIC

A few days after my tea party, an Army Veteran (AKA Owl) caught up with me on the trail. He was my age, but with a slighter build. My pace was slower than most because I put more thought into foot placement to prevent injury. As we walked, I had diarrhea of the mouth and exclaimed, "I'm the most talkative of my family."

"It's no wonder—how could they get a word in edgewise."

A strained silence fell over us for an uncomfortable two minutes before I started in again. In my ramblings, I asked, "Why did God pick me? I'm not politically connected, rich, or a good speaker."

"Don't worry. He knows what He's doing, picking the right Catholic with all the guilt you carry."

Laughing weakly at myself, I imagined God saying, What? Well, forgive Me for having a sense of humor. Anyway, you don't need to be skilled, just available; I'll do the rest.

Owl raised beef for a living and didn't talk much about himself, though I was not sure if it was because I did more talking than listening. He seemed to have a protective shield that, on the surface, looked like it was meant to prevent people from coming in. In reality, it prevented him from getting out.

During our (mostly one-sided) conversations, I repeated what someone had told me: "You can't look into another person's eyes for a minute and a half and not love them." After I said that, he wouldn't even look at my face (how sad—to fear loving someone that much). After three days of hiking together, I detoured to spend a night in town.

Fear takes many forms and it seemed all of mine stopped me from being free, who I was born to be and I got to see myself in Owl. This inspired Challenge 9. This one has been the greatest stumbling block for most people taking our challenges, how will you do on this one? In the back of the book all the challenges are listed for you to take your own inward journey.

MIKE

Trying to atone for the guilt of not saving the Marines I'd served with (and the ones currently at war) brought up the same emotion I had experienced as a kid with my brother Mike.

One summer morning, I watched him throw pea gravel from the driveway at the green wooden shingles of our house, which my father built himself. He did it to hear the sound, like driving rain on a tin roof, and I was there because it was my job to watch him.

Without any warning, Dad exploded out of the house, grabbed Mike by the arm, picked him up off the ground, and beat him with a stick. He still had some pebbles in his hand, which were embedded into his palms as he tried to cover his ass. I just stood there paralyzed in fear, wondering if I'd be next.

Now, seeing through the eyes of an adult, I was watching an eight-year-old child protecting his four-year-old brother from a 220-pound drunk adult's unprovoked attack. What could I have done? It was over before I could move.

I have carried the guilt of not defending my brother, being taught to always protect my siblings no matter the cost—just as I was taught to go back for the wounded in the Marines. Reflecting on this story enabled me to forgive myself for what I had failed to do so long ago.

IT DIDN'T AFFECT ME

When I returned to the trail, after a day to rest my feet, I came upon a woman heading north. Most hikers head north; I was one of the few heading south. Having calculated how long the trail would take to complete at my pace, I didn't want to get stuck in a blizzard on the north end.

She asked what I was doing. After I explained why I was walking barefoot, she said, "My father was in World War II, but it didn't affect him." She took a breath and continued, "At restaurants, he has to see a window and keep his back to the wall because he has to know he can get out. He was in a bunker during the war. He wouldn't celebrate Thanksgiving because he saw natives digging through the garbage for food."

Sometimes we try to protect ourselves from the truth.

After a reflective pause, she concluded, "I guess it did affect him."

I wondered if she would ever think about how it may have affected her.

Sometimes we try to protect ourselves from the truth.

UNCONVENTIONAL 20-YEAR-OLD

In an attempt to pace myself after long days up and down mountains, I slept under the stars instead of heading to a three-sided shelter. The shelters were spaced about 10 to 15 miles apart. I had only walked about eight and wasn't a fan of walking in the dark, being unable to see the obstacles on the ground and increasing the risk of getting lost. Sometimes the trail wasn't clearly marked; even during the day, there were times I veered off. Unable to predict the rain better than a weather forecaster, I preferred shelters. Turns out they were drier than my homemade tent (a conglomeration of string, straps, buckles, tent poles, Tyvek, and tape), but pushing on through those extra miles to get to one was counterproductive, as it meant my body wouldn't be able to recuperate enough to keep up with my mind.

It was raining the following day as I passed through a rocky section where the Appalachian Trail maintenance crew was working to keep the trail marked and clear while rearranging rocks to prevent erosion, an endless task considering much of the trail passes through mountain ranges.

"Every time I see you, it's raining," I said. They laughed, covered head to toe with mud.

I spoke with one young volunteer whose father had PTSD from the Gulf War. It hurt to hear his story and see how it affected him: body slumped, shoulders sagged, head lowered. His tone was melancholic as he stared at the ground, remembering the man he had admired—once a tall oak, now reduced to kindling. There was a heaviness and maturity about the boy that didn't match the conventional 20-year-old impression. He shouldn't have to worry about a 40-year-old man that could take his life at any moment.

DAD'S WAR

Watching "Combat" (a TV show in the '60s about an outfit fighting in WWII) as a kid and thinking about how fun and exciting it'd be to engage in a war, I asked my dad questions any eleven-year-old would ask. "What was it like? What did you do? Did you get shot? Were you afraid? Did you kill anyone?"

He would tell me little bits and pieces: getting hit in the ass with a piece of shrapnel, watching 12-year-olds from the Wolf Pack (the name given to Hitler's youth used as soldiers at the end of the war) executed, listening to heavy artillery firing through the nights (and not knowing which was worse—being on patrol or sleeping under the canons, the likely cause of his TBI[2]), and washing his hands with soap that was rumored to be made from the remains of Jews and Poles. My father was at Auschwitz after the liberation as one of many troop members encouraged by Eisenhower to visit the liberated camps and bear witness to the atrocities that happened there.

He was afraid for his life every day he was in combat. I asked again, "Did you kill anyone?" He got that faraway look and spoke just above a whisper, talking like he was in a dream, about how he shot at a man and wasn't sure if he had died.

I got scared. Sitting before me was a man that I feared—a man I thought wasn't afraid of anything. He disappeared before my eyes into a shadow. I never asked again.

――――――――――

[2] Survivors of a traumatic brain injury (TBI) can face effects lasting for a few days or for the rest of their lives. Their challenges may include impaired brain functionality, movement, visual or auditory sensations, and emotion control. The Defense and Veterans Brain Injury Center (DVBIC) reports that more than 50 percent of injuries sustained during the conflicts in Iraq and Afghanistan are the result of explosives. A complex pressure wave, called an over-pressurization wave, is generated by the explosion, resulting in an instantaneous rise in atmospheric pressure, much higher than normal, too high for humans to withstand.

TRAIL TRIVIA

There are "thru-hikers" (those going the whole distance), "section hikers" (those just doing a portion of the trail), and "day hikers" (those committing to only a day or two). There is a huge difference between these three. Most thru-hikers talk about food, gear, and their feet because they can never eat enough to maintain their weight, their gear is all they have and their feet always hurt. They usually have a stronger odor, and most are pretty laid back after the first month.

There are purists that only walk the "white blazes" (white-marked AT) and others that may use "blue blazes" (shortcuts). Then there are those that use yellow blazes (the highway). I'm not a purist, but I didn't do any yellow blazing.

Thru-hikers usually have a trail name, which they give themselves or receive from other hikers. Being curious, I asked hikers their trail name and found it entertaining. One name I found particularly curious was Cornbread.

"Why?" I asked Cornbread.

"Because I like it," he said.

"Oh, mine is Tyvek because I made all my gear fr..."

He stopped me mid-sentence. "We know what you call yourself, but that's not what we call you."

"Really, what do you call me?"

"We call you the 'Holy Shit Man, how does he do it?'"

Which I shortened to "Holy Shit Man," which is what I heard every time I came upon unsuspecting hikers.

I liked theirs more than the name I gave myself. A few others I really liked were Face Plant (he fell down face first), Sees Bears Everywhere (she was afraid of bears, so every shadow or stump was a bear), and C.S. (a woman had lanced a blister on his foot and, when it burst, she cried out, "Just like a cum shot!").

Gear took on its own personality traits. By the end of the walk, my gear was mistaken for garbage whenever I left it on the ground. It had a tear strength of 10/12 lbs. With Tyvek tape on it, its strength was multiplied several times and could be exposed to the elements for 9 months and remain useful.

It was put to the acid test by serving as my landing pad when I would slip and land on my back, constantly being taken on and off, loaded and reloaded, and being exposed to all weather. I was amazed at how well it had held up for so long. Whatever area wasn't taped disintegrated due to exposure and abuse, but the taped areas still held together.

One of the questions that often came up when I ran into another hiker was, "Are you a thru-hiker?" While on the trail, I wrote a poem in response to this question:

Are You a Thru-hiker?

Does it matter that I massage the naked spine
Of Mother Earth with my feet
Or Her asphalt-plastered face with rubber

Does it matter that my hike began
At birth and ends with my death
Where She will embrace me once again

For She judges not
She knows the walk is not about the walk
It is about what happens on the walk

She judges not with glaring signs nor
Subtle messages
That I am not enough

She allows me to be
By being
Allows me to remember

By knowing
There is only one of us
On the trail

I see my reflection
In all of you
If I see something I don't like

I change it
When I see what I like
I embrace it

Children show me who
I am
Honey Moon Sue shows me

I am more!
Than I think I am
Angels show me

What I can be
No I am not finished hiking
I am but hiking through this way

"We call you the 'Holy Shit Man, how does he do it?'"

VET'S ON THE TRAIL

I came up to a river that was normally fordable, but that day it was swollen to the point hikers had to be brought across by canoe. While waiting, I met Gunny, a Marine who reminded me of Sgt. Rock from the comics—he just needed a cigar and a helmet. He was covered with visible scars of 'man-killing-man in a rage of hate and fear.' Most simply refer to it as war.

I shouldn't have been surprised by the number of Veterans on the trail trying to find peace. They simply thought of it before me. It's our version of a 'Vision Quest' to find the answers only we have. Some go from one end to the other, then turn around to repeat it or find an area and stick around.

Many of us steal the time to figure out who we were before entering the military—to find that part that had belonged—because we were so far from home we didn't know who that was. I knew I'd run into him if I stayed out there long enough, waging the battle to overcome myself.

A lot of the people walking the trail are Veterans that are intentionally taking the time and making the effort to care for themselves, because on some level they know that they need this as part of their walk home, maybe as a rite of passage. Therefore inspiring Challenge 4. In the back of the book all the challenges are listed for you to take your own inward journey.

POST-DISCHARGE: YEAR ONE

After meeting Gunny and being ferried across the river, I daydreamed about when I got discharged and was coming home on a train to Hampton Bays. We were packed in like sardines. Someone called me a baby killer in a voice just above a whisper, blending in with the sounds of the track against racing wheels turning round and round. I couldn't believe my ears; they didn't even know me or what I did. I was on their side and had stayed stateside. I never even went over.

I scanned the vain crowd. None of them could keep their eyes off the reflection they sought on polished shoes. I never found that brave soul who spoke under their breath, even after I yelled out loud, "Who said that!" They all yelled back with their silence, "It was I!"

I did different jobs, saving money, to live the rest of my life in a cabin on the land I bought while in the Merchant Marines (1968-1969). Getting out of the service in 1972, I went back into the woods. . Everyone (back then we were called Hippies because of long hair, attire, and percieved lifestyle of sex, drugs, and rock 'n roll) that lived there with me was gone, driven off by the locals who were 50 years behind the times where I came from on Long Island. They probably feared we were a bad influence on their children—a subverse element in their community—or they just wanted to burn houses down and drive people that weren't born there out.

In fact, the townspeople had burnt down five houses in the past year but left mine alone because I had been in the Marine Corps. Maybe they were just scared of me. Being there by myself were the happiest days I had had in a long time—nobody telling me what to do, and I didn't have to make anyone else happy.

It went well until tax time. It was only $99, but it may as well have been a million. I would have to go back to Long Island to make the money, as the only job available to me was picking strawberries at 50 cents an hour. It had been easy to be peaceful when I was alone in the woods, not having to deal with people; I was perfect when I got my way. When I first got home from the military, I thought people had changed. In reality, it wasn't them; it was me.

Going back to Long Island to work, I figured I'd need more than $99 to stay up there. I found work moving and framing houses and was able to save some money. I decided to use my GI bill to go to college. My decision to go back to school was mainly because I felt inferior to college students, which I later realized was ridiculous because the majority had the magnified innocent arrogance of high school kids who never had to make it on their own.

To the untrained eye, my plan worked well—except I started to drink more; of course that wasn't really much of a problem for me.

I thought people had changed.
In reality, it wasn't them; it was me.

MOUNT AVERY

It was a bright, sun-shiny day as I walked over Bigelow Mountain's Avery Peak (4,090'elv.) and West Peak (4,145'elv.). It was the most torturous set of stones I had ever set my feet on (besides the stone floor of divorce court). The rocks seemed like they were 40 grit or coarser, etched in acid and busted up from boulder to pea-size by a chain gang wielding sledge-hammers.

You didn't want to slip, slide or drag your feet since just lightly grazing the top of one toe tore the skin off. Over the course of six hours, I mastered the form of Polish Tai Chi, carefully choreographing my steps to align with my unmovable partners at a blistering half a mile an hour.

RECON MARINE

Upon arriving at the Stranton Motel, I requested, "a Recon Marine Captain for a bunk."

The owner simply replied, "Hi, Tyvek, there's no charge for Marines here. I served from 1982 to 1989. Thanks for what you're doing."

I was still for a moment as it sunk in that, for the past 33 years, I'd tried to deny that part of me by not telling people I was a Marine, wanting to forget the memories of that era. Unable to outrun the past, I now embraced it because he accepted that part of me, taking away the past 33 years in an instant simply by caring. Being a Marine will always be a part of who I am.

Being a Marine will always be a part of who I am.

TONY

I joined the Marines at the age of 19 with my childhood friend Tony. Our friendship was forged in the hell of two alcoholic fathers (Veterans) and our attempts to survive in that environment. We lived a street away from one another. When we first met, I asked, "How old are you?"

"How old are you?"

We both said, "six," and that was all we needed to know—we had something in common. Little did we know at that moment, we had much more in common than age.

It was a time where you went outside to play till dark or your parents called your name out the back door. The first day we played together, we were squirting one another with my dad's water hose when Tony grabbed it and whirled it around like a lasso. I tried to get it back, it hit me in the head, and we both went frantic—me to get the hose shut off before my father found out and Tony because my head was bleeding, which he still apologizes for.

We grew up doing what most kids do—nothing and stuff. We built a tree fort when we were nine, but it didn't last long. We were playing with matches one cold day and burnt it down, setting the woods on fire in the process. We tried to keep it from spreading, but then the fire whistle blew.

Tony looked at me and said, "My old man will kill me if he finds out."

"Mine too, but I'm staying."

Tony took off and I tried to put it out by myself while the neighbors watched, none of whom stepped forward to help. Then I saw my mother storming up the path from our house with a fire all her own. She grabbed my arm like she wanted to pull it out of its socket and dragged me home. Her voice trembled with rage and embarrassment. "Wait till your father gets home."

I laid in bed and the only thing on my mind was the beating I was about to get. I heard him come home and listened to my mother yell for him to punish me after telling him what happened. There was a moment of silence. Then he came, slowly opened the door, and looked at me.

I couldn't look him in the eye—I was too scared and ashamed. He stared for half a second and said, "I think you've been punished enough." Then he closed the door. I heard my mother yelling furiously through the walls, but I was so relieved that I fell asleep.

That was the first and last time my father never beat me for something I did—probably because I stayed to put the fire out, but I'll never know for sure. Several times before she died, my mother asked me to forgive her for how angry she was. I always forgave her, but I think she never forgave herself.

Unfortunately, Tony's father found out and he did get a beating, but that didn't end it for Tony and me. When we were older, we got .22s and shot rats at the dump and did target practice at the beach. One day, a bullet ricocheted off the water and went through someone's window while they were in the room. That resulted in a visit to the police station.

We started drinking at age 11, which was around the time Tony's dad died from cirrhosis—so he didn't suffer those extreme disciplinary actions (dished out by his Veteran father who purportedly picked up pieces of men and put them in buckets during WWII) to keep him in check.

We got into boxing. Tony was always a little bigger, stronger, and faster than me, and he stuck with it. The last time he fought in the ring, he was 45 and he placed second in the lightweight division of the Texarkana Toughman competition.

I used to go into houses without breaking or stealing anything—just wanting to look around. I showed one of our friends, who wanted to steal. Since I wouldn't, they went without me. That's when Tony and I started to run in different circles. They finally got caught, but the turning point for Tony was when he and a few others burned down the beach pavilion in town. He "went away" while I stayed and graduated.

When Tony got back, we reconnected and won the draft lottery. His number was 16 and mine was 34. Tony decided to beat the draft by joining the Marine Corps because they would take him with a record (19-year-old Polish logic at work). When he first asked me to sign up with him, I refused. "I'll wait for the FBI to come and get me." I wasn't going after what I had seen and learned in the Merchant Marines—plus I believed killing was a sin that I wouldn't commit.

Nevertheless, he persisted, and I finally decided it would be a great way to punish my parents for hypocrisy—why waste those passive-aggressive techniques I had mastered so well?

MARINE TRAINING

When I told my parents about joining the Marines, my father looked at me like he knew a secret he wouldn't share and my mother asked, "Why? You don't believe in killing..."

"It must be okay because the church doesn't stop it and I want to experience it—see what it's like to kill someone."

My mother cried. Wishing I could take back those words (no matter what I thought about the church and every other form of authority they believed in), my heart turned to lead and I watched in silence.

On the bus to boot camp, traveling through acres of military equipment, seeing hundreds of trainees, I thought, We really kill people and I still really believe it's wrong. How can we do this? Weren't we taught our whole lives that it's wrong—a sin for which we'd go to hell, regardless of the excuse? It seemed insane that I hoped to survive my time in the USMC without killing anyone.

Dying never really crossed my mind until my sister sent me a letter with black and white balloons, symbolizing the dead and those who would die. I sat there quietly wondering if I'd be one of them.

At my first duty station, I got into an altercation with my Commanding Officer (CO). I guess my day at "Motivation" (an attitude-adjustment program) during boot camp hadn't stuck. Skipping my first inspection (because I didn't feel like going and no one was going to tell me what to do) resulted in my own private inspection after I was found doing laundry instead of waiting obediently with my shoes and foot locker. At this impromptu meeting, my CO informed me that we would have a bloody fight, which he confidently stated I would lose.

"Oh yeah?" I responded, just as confident—with a sarcastic undertone of surprise.

Not too many days after that, I was on duty guarding missiles when we had our next encounter. When he made his presence known, I unholstered my .45, which was within the parameters of my duty. Being overzealous, I took it upon myself to interpret the manual the best I could by holding the .45 next to his head (there was no clear description as to how or where to hold the weapon). I did this while smiling (which wasn't covered either, but I thought it was a nice touch). I watched as beads of sweat formed on his head, saturating his military-issued high-and-tight haircut, joining in streams that dribbled down his face and off his chin.

He took one fearful glance at me, quickly signed the logbook, and confirmed all the missiles were accounted for. We did our salute and he was off to change his linen. Within two weeks, I received orders with five others to go to Vietnam.

He won.

However, before going on leave, I was required to visit the commander. I assumed he didn't want to miss the opportunity to gloat. Stepping into his spartan office through a plain wooden door, I noticed the sergeant-at-arms was present. The commander asked, "What do you think of that, Zaleski?"

"The only way you're getting me over there is if you chain me to a helicopter."

"Is that right?

"That's right."

We talked a bit about his son who wanted to join the Merchant Marines, which I knew all about, having been in when I was 17 and 18.

He asked, "Does it makes a man out of you?"

"If you're not one when you go in, you won't be one when you get out." My definition of being a man was honoring your word and convictions. I didn't ask his, assuming it was universal, but maybe I gave him too much credit.

Upon arriving home, I shared my orders with no one, still regretting having hurt my mother. In my bedroom, I got down on my knees and prayed, "God, I don't know if I have the courage to not kill another man. I'm afraid and want to live. If I don't shoot, will I endanger the lives of my fellow Marines? If I do, how can I go to heaven? What do I do? Help me!"

I considered retreating to Canada but decided that was cowardly. I would suffer the consequences of my actions and do five years in a military prison or face a firing squad for disobeying direct orders. I hoped it wouldn't be the firing squad (how ironic—afraid to die in combat by not killing someone only to die home where I didn't have to).

I arrived at Camp Pendleton, where the other five men were shipped out by the clerk. I told the man in a cracked voice, "I'm not going," as thoughts of being killed stateside for my convictions raced through my head.

"Don't worry, you coward. Your orders have been changed."

I exhaled a deep breath of relief, like letting the air out of a balloon about to pop, as I silently thanked God. Maybe I should've thanked my Commanding Officer, but I didn't think he had anything to do with it then. Now, maybe.

With no immediate orders, I was interviewed and asked if I was a conscientious objector. "What's that?" I asked.

"Do you believe we kill people?"

"Yes, but I don't believe in killing."

"That's not what I asked."

After the interview, I was sent to the barracks where young men, screaming in their sleep, awaited the determination of which discharge they would receive: Dishonorable, General, or Section 8 (mentally unfit).

With all that time on our hands, we wrestled to see who was the strongest. I used to think I was pretty bad because I wouldn't back down; I would've fought anyone. There was one Marine given a wide berth by the others, but no one explained why I shouldn't mess with him—they just told me to watch out because he was bad. Being me, I had to find out for myself, so I befriended the wiry southerner getting out on a Section 8. One night, when we went camping just outside the barracks, I asked him, "What makes you so bad?"

He looked through me with crystal blue eyes, a wolf looking at his next meal, and said, "You can't stay awake forever."

I wasn't bad. That guy was bad; there was something missing when I looked into his eyes—the ability to feel. They were empty of vulnerability and compassion.

After two weeks, I was assigned duty as a clerk typist and remained at that base for the rest of my two-year contract. I was just doing my time, waiting to get out, still overwhelmed with the part I played in the machinery of war. At times, I would awaken not knowing who or where I was.

A month before my discharge, I met one of the five men with whom I was originally supposed to go to Vietnam. He was limping, and I asked what happened.

"We all got shot. Two are dead."

It flipped a switch. Feelings of guilt, grief, anger, shame, and fear slapped me across the face. My thoughts raced. Was standing up for my convictions the right thing to do? Am I a coward? A hypocrite? Should I have been there? Could I have saved them? What did they suffer for? Die for? Should I be dead? My mind whirled with that litany till I forced myself to shut it all down, focusing on the anger and propelling it outward.

Shortly after getting out, I stopped wearing shoes as a memorial for them. I wanted to believe they had died for my freedom and I honored that by not wearing shoes. At the time, I didn't realize it was a way to continue being angry—just an act of defiance, as I told no one why I was doing it.

I told myself my anger was a result of feeling that I was free to do only what they told me I could do and that nobody cared about anything but themselves and money. I became a coward because I was afraid to be free—to make a choice and be responsible for it.

———◆•◆•◆———

The only way you're getting me over there
is if you chain me to a helicopter

PARADISE

Walking from white marker to white marker, I was immersed in the rawness of a chilling wind. The morning sky looked like it wanted to snow as if to remind me of its unpredictability. (It could, if it so desired, but because of my expectations, it wouldn't.) I took a detour to Paradise (a motel owned by a WWII Polish refugee) that rated high among thru-hikers.

Upon arrival, I left my gear alongside the building when I saw the door was closed with a "be back later" sign and went into town to get food and send what I had journaled to my ex-wife to put on the website I'd created for my walk. Returning for my gear, I met two other hikers: Easy and Pepper.

"Are you Tyvek?" Easy asked.

"Yes."

They each shook my hand, and Pepper said, "We have been trying to catch up to you for a month. We both just got out of the Marines after doing five deployments."

They got on the trail within a month of getting out and, because of trouble adjusting to home, thought thru-hiking would be a good way to ease in. They told me the Transition Awareness Program (TAP) during debriefing was basically just instructions on how to write a resume.

They were asked to raise their hand if they had a problem with PTSD. It was the shortest part of the program. Here's a thought: *What 20-year-old, trained to be a machine, is going to ask for help in front of their peers?*

We talked about war and politics. I thought the news only told me what they wanted me to know, as if they made the news instead of reporting it, so I was interested in the true perspective.

"I swore I wouldn't talk politics," Pepper said, "The next guy that tells me why I'm fighting, I'm going to kill him. What do they know about the war, watching CNN? I am over there doing it and they have no solutions to offer." I felt stupid being clueless as to what was really going on.

Later that evening, Easy pulled me aside and said, "I have killed men, women, and children—young and old. Am I going to hell?"

I was stunned. Nobody had ever asked for my opinion. I had always given it freely, so it had no value. At that moment, though, what

I said mattered. I prayed to myself. *God, help me. I don't know what to say. You do it.*

I looked at Easy and said, "You're not going to hell. You did nothing wrong, but it doesn't matter what I say if you don't believe it." He was quiet for a moment, and then I listened to his story, hoping there was some way to lift this immense burden off him.

He told me that his grandfather was a WWII Marine Master Sergeant in the Pacific and died when Easy's father was in his twenties. There had been a lot of bad blood between his father and grandfather. "I think my dad blamed his troubled relationship with his father on the Marine Corps."

Easy's father didn't want him to enlist, but he did anyway, using those passive-aggressive tools we pick up to get back at our parents for their differences. After serving, he understood why his father hadn't wanted him to go. We realized that we were not too different as we talked about what had driven us to do the things we had done.

I told him, "You may think I'm crazy, but I want to tell you about a dream I had, real as me sitting here in front of you."

In my teens, going to Catholic Church every Sunday with my parents, incense burning, and Latin prayers hammering the sermon home, I sat on uncomfortable hardwood benches, bored out of my skull. One sermon, in particular, stood out to me. The priest said, "If Christ were here today, or if we were there then, we couldn't stop his crucifixion. It was ordained." Smugly smirking to myself, I thought, *I could stop it.*

After falling asleep that night, I found myself kneeling on dirt, hard-packed by hundreds of feet. I felt the rawness of the pre-dawn air, tasted the dust kicked up by sandaled soldiers, and smelled their wine-soaked sweat, ripe from the night before. I was totally present, aware of everything around me, and full of self-righteous power because, at that moment, I was about to help torture a man to death—a man I was led to believe was evil.

Being in total control over another life was a drug that gave me the power of God. Hammering the last nail into his hand, I was so intent that I never even looked at his face—just the iron spike driving into his flesh. In the back of my mind, however, I knew something wasn't quite right.

I hesitated before getting up, realizing I didn't hear him begging for his life; I didn't smell fear, that acid that should have etched the air. The sandaled foot the centurion had planted on the man's wrist to hold his hand still remained in place as I knelt up and peered his eyes. He looked through me, into my soul, and whispered, "I love you."

That instant, I knew what I had done was wrong. I went insane, yelling, screaming, and hitting him and everything within reach of the hammer tightly clasped in my hand.

I got up and ran, blinded by tears and racked with grief. I awoke with a painful thud as I dashed into the bedroom wall, screaming with snot running down my face and sweat-soaked sheets stuck to my body, not knowing which world I was in. I stood there scared, remembering that I had gone to bed on Long Island in 1963.

I had kept the dream a secret for a long time, questioning my sanity over it. How could I have done such a thing? What kind of monster was I? Would I ever be forgiven? How could I make it right? Was it real?

"I know," Easy said after hearing my story, "I have dreams too."

How long will their walk be? Will they ever make it home or will they just be visitors?

The following are two of the poems Easy gave me, printed with his permission:

Poem Number One by Easy

In the depths of the maze,
My thoughts run in a million different ways

I'm here, at night I cry
I think I'm livin' just to die

My mind's dead, I'm fallin' apart
My woman holds the key to my heart

She's my angel, she's my hope
She guides my way, she's how I cope

If it wasn't for her, I'd be a wreck
She's my guardian, step by step

I love you freak, I really do
I love you so much, I'd kill for you

Anything you want, I'll give to you
Just keep truckin' with me baby
We'll get through
I'm F____ up sittin'
At this bar, just missin'
YOU!

Poem Number Two by Easy

Let my demons run free
Please God help me

I search and seek
But I know I'm a lost sheep

Please Lord, help me find my way
I'm jacked up, I've lost—wandered astray
I beg for your help, but I don't expect it
I try to live your rules, but
I don't respect 'em

I'm going to hell, and I know this
Take me willingly, I won't resist

———◆———

What 20-year-old, trained to be a machine, is going to ask for help in front of their peers?

MOUNT WASHINGTON

I left Paradise early the next morning, slowly transitioning from civilization to woodland at the pace of water dripping out of a leaky faucet. I finally reached a shelter to avoid sleeping on the ground in the rain that pounded the earth with the sound of a muffled drum.

Having slept through the night, I arose as silence got a second wind. It was hard to force myself out of a warm, dry sleeping bag, but at least it was easier than extracting myself from a wet sack as if I were a market fish wrapped in soggy paper.

I enjoyed a breakfast of champions (granola in hot choc-olate) and pushed on to Pinkham Notch (2,050'elv.), heading towards Mount Washington (6,288'elv.). What awaited was a location known for some of the most severe weather in the US on account of three fronts converging in one spot. The weather there can change from a warm sunny day to a blinding blizzard in double digits below zero with winds in excess of 100 mph within the span of a heartbeat (or maybe three). Ill-prepared people have died there by being overconfident of their skills or discounting Mother Nature, both of which happened to be my *modus operandi* (MO).

At the base of Mount Washington, where it was warm and sunny, I met Mike, who hiking with his three sons (sixteen, nine, and seven). We climbed together and I talked with them about why I was doing the hike barefoot.

Mike asked, "What do I do for my boys?"

"You're doing it. You're giving them the two most precious things you have: you and your time. Support them in whatever they do and let them know you will always love them no matter what they have done, though it doesn't mean you have to like what they've done."

Our eyes locked in silence, filling a gap that would take a lifetime of discussion to complete; I felt his passion and under-stood we shared the same struggle. We cried without words, embraced, and went our separate ways. In my silent walking, the heavy words of our short exchange wrapped around me, blocking out all other thoughts.

THE BRAWL

Just like Mike, I also questioned, *What do I do for my boys?*

In 1998, I had attended an empowerment seminar at Life Spring (which later spawned Momentum) that had had a huge impact on me—it essentially took me out of victim mode and changed my priorities by removing money from the top of my list. If it did that for me, what could it do for my sons? It would be one of the greatest gifts I could give them—one that couldn't be stolen by time or people—to live from a place of power and self-worth.

Going to seminars geared towards making more money was no problem for me, even though I was financially secure. When it came to learning about myself, though, I thought there was nothing wrong with me—that I didn't need to learn anything. There was a time in my life when going to a self-empowerment seminar would be like admitting there was something wrong with me instead of just being a way to get more out of life. So, when my oldest son Zach turned 18, I told him he was going to the seminar to achieve his potential.

"Who are you to tell me what to do?"

I rephrased it and asked, "Would you do it for me?"

"Yes."

Towards the end of the graduation ceremony, lights low and music playing, the seminar graduates closed their eyes. When the lights came on, they opened their eyes to see the people that got them to the seminar standing in front of them. When Zach opened his eyes and saw me, he cried, I cried, we hugged, and he thanked me for the gift.

Four years later, when my youngest son Adam turned 18, I politely asked him to go. He looked at me, laughed, and said, "If you tie me up." I attributed his hostility to him taking the divorce personally and his mother filling him with poison about me, but at this moment, I was more concerned with the impact on his life.

"If I beat you in a fight, will you go?" This seemed logical since I owned a gym and had the matchmaker for the Ultimate Fighting Championship (UFC) running the dojo where we had both trained together (it was a male bonding thing).

"Yeah, and you don't even have to wear a gi."

Anyone that fights in mixed martial arts knows that would be a huge advantage, so he was pretty sure he was going to kick the shit out of me and was thrilled by the opportunity to do so.

"Okay, give me a month to train and we'll fight when you come back from Colorado."

He would be staying with his mom while on break from the University of Southampton, lying on her couch, watching TV, and eating ice cream. I would be training like an animal and practicing one move to end it quickly.

When the day of the fight came, Adam's interview was videoed, as well as the fight (he wanted this ass-kicking saved for posterity) by Bob, another fighter we had befriended.

He was asked, "What do you think?"

"Ha! I'm going to tear his arms out and beat him over the head with them."

He asked, "Is there anything you're worried about?"

"If I don't take him out right away, it's going to be a long hard fight because he has endurance like no one I know."

When asked if he'd give me a rematch if I lost, he said, "Sure."

When Bob interviewed me and asked what I thought about the fight, I told him, "He's younger, faster, and stronger than me. If I don't beat him, it's my own fault that I didn't train hard enough."

When asked if I would give him a rematch if he lost, I said, "Sure, but if I lose, I don't deserve a rematch because it would mean I didn't train hard enough."

Before we started the fight, Adam took one look at me and I could see some doubt in his eyes. Guess my training paid off. He changed his mind about the gi. There would be no kicking, punching, or biting—just holds. When we started, I raced in but hesitated. He reversed the hold I had been working on to end it quickly and almost took me out.

As the fight progressed, I had him in nine finishing holds but would release him each time because I didn't want to hurt him. I thought to myself, *I'll just stop*, but then I heard that little voice inside of me ask, *If you stop, do you think he'll go?*

No.

Well, you better finish him.

I got him in a hold where I thought I had broken his arm. In that position, we locked eyes and he tapped out with one finger. As soon as I released him, he cried.

I closed my eyes and thought I had won, but the truth was, I lost. He looked at me in angry defeat and said, "Don't worry, you just hurt my pride. I'll go."

After the fight, he asked me if I could close my hands. I tried and couldn't. "I can't either." We had fought for 38 and a half minutes nonstop. He immediately asked for a rematch the next day, which I gave him. It lasted almost a minute. He beat me with a vengeance. I didn't need to win; I already had. Plus, I was still whipped from fighting the day before. I was also glad that it wasn't my oldest son Zach who had fought me; he could have beaten both of us.

Adam completed the empowerment seminar. When he opened his eyes and saw me at the graduation ceremony, he said defiantly, "Don't think you're going to get me to cry. Just be happy I went," poking his finger in my chest.

I held up my hands, "Okay."

He wouldn't give me any details, but I noticed he had the edge of a lawn mower blade after cutting a yard of gravel.

A year later, I attended a party given by the founder of Momentum. When I was introduced to Adam's trainer, her eyes went wide. "You're Adam Zaleski's father!?"

After I confirmed the connection, she asked, "Did he tell you what happened?"

"No."

"At the start of the training, we break the ice by asking everyone how they got here. Most say a parent or spouse really loves them and just paid for it."

She relayed to me that my son, who I knew to be as talkative as a cigar store Indian, stood up and said, "My father beat me up to get me here." A dramatic pause stretched out the hush before he added, "That's how I know how much he loves me."

How far would you go for the one you love? How much time would you spend and what language would you speak so they could hear you? I asked a girl once, "How far would you go on a first date?"

She replied, "Mexico."

Me too.

I sent a copy of this chapter to my son for approval. He responded by telling me there were things he would never forgive me for. I wrote back saying I hoped he would be able to someday. That night, as I told my girlfriend what Adam said, I laughed because I was asking or expecting him to do something I hadn't done: forgive myself.

I put off writing this book for nearly a decade, telling myself I was just lazy. In truth, I was simply afraid, wanting to believe the lies I had made up about myself, not wanting to see who I really was. Putting thoughts to print might kill this hazy version I had of myself, showing me who I really was. Would it make all those years a lie? Would it be too much work? Too uncomfortable? Or was I just afraid of how powerful I really was—to create change in myself and in the world? Had I wasted my life, taking what looked like the easy path to the untrained eye?

At first, I thought it was done, letting my sons know about the motivation for my walks because I had the journals I wrote while on my walks. It would be nice for my sons to know who I was and understand why I did it, but writing this book forced me to crawl under the bed to see what was there. Thinking I would see a monster, I only saw a scared man who believed he was a monster. The good news is, it's a mistake I'm currently rectifying—not a sin for which there is no correction.

In truth, I was simply afraid

This brawl was much more than just reaching out to a family member and is part of the reason for Challenges 5, and 8. How far would you go to let someone know you care about them, would your actions match the overused phrase, "I love you more than anything in the world." In the back of the book all the challenges are listed for you to take your own inward journey.

DEPLETED URANIUM

After leaving Mike and his sons, I continued to the top of Mount Washington. I was blown to the ground several times in 80 mph gusts of snow before reaching the indoor shelter. It might as well have been the Ritz-Cartlon with its four walls and heat. I spent a comfortable night there and departed the next morning.

When I left the higher elevations of Mount Washington, I was back to sleeping on the earth, separated by only one layer of felt and a piece of Tyvek. I got up each morning and swore I never slept, yet felt rested and wondered how that could be. Truth is, I knew I had actually slept because everyone around me told me I snored through the entire night.

A day hiker asked, "Why don't you support the cause to stop using depleted uranium[3] because of the effects it has on the troops?"

After her long-winded spiel, I said, "Sounds great. What have you done so far about it?"

After a few moments of silence, she said, "Nothing."

"Well, that's how much I will support you, seeing how important it is to you." She got pissed, turned around and walked away.

She reminded me of when I would, unasked, give someone my ideas for helping others, hoping they would do it because there wasn't any money in it for me (and I even had the nerved to be annoyed when they didn't do it!). It was eye-opening to stand on the other side of the fence; the view was completely different.

In the area I was walking, everywhere there was a trail marker, there was a pile of moose droppings (they must have thought it was a bathroom sign). I looked ahead and saw what I thought was a boulder in the middle of the trail, but then it moved; it was a moose.

It took one look at me and stood up. It was huge—at least seven feet from the ground to the top of its back. My first thought was, *Oh my God, it has a velvet couch on its head.* After looking more closely, though, I saw it was a rack over six feet across with felt still on it. The moose walked

---

[3] Depleted uranium is the element left over from the extraction process of obtaining U-235 (mainly U-238, which isn't as radioactive, but very effective for tips of shells). It is over two times denser than steel, has more momentum, penetrates as well as it ignites, and it disintegrates after penetration.

(not ran) away, hardly making a sound as it melted into the woods where the trees were only two feet apart.

It confirmed more to me that there must be a Sasquatch School for all animals. I swore that bears must attend such a school. Sometimes, as I walked on the trail, I would see them out of the corner of my eye, like a shadow. Other times, they would make me aware of their presence by making the noise of an electric bulldozer.

———◆•◆•◆———

It was eye-opening to stand on the other side
of the fence; the view was completely different.

DO MY FEET HURT?

People asked me all the time if my feet hurt. One day, I finally answered one inquirer with, "Yes, my feet hurt."

"Put some shoes on, stupid." That was the last time I complained.

One memorable afternoon on the trail, I tramped through what seemed like an eternity of acorns on hard-packed dirt (half a mile or more). If I had been blindfolded, I would have thought I was walking over marbles on a hardwood floor.

My Turkish friends told me that one of the ways they tortured people back home was to put a phone book (not the NY edition) on the bottom of a prisoner's feet and beat it with a Billy club. There are over 7,000 nerve endings in each foot, affecting the whole body. That day, walking over acorns was Turkish torture; my whole body ached.

That night, I dragged myself to a hostel for a zero-day (a day without walking). I laid on my back, giving my feet a chance to catch up to the rest of my body. I had to do this every five days or so because I couldn't pace myself to simply walk 8 hours a day (which my body could handle). Some days required a break, especially after occasions like acorn torture.

Every morning, my feet spoke to me of abuse and violations. After half an hour of slow walking, though, their stiffness lessened and they would start feeling better—either that or I quit listening to them.

Because of the constant rotation of being wet and dry, the natural oils were leached out of my feet. They split, cracked, and bled. I started coating them with "bag balm," a Vaseline-like ointment used on cow utters. If it was good enough for cows' tits, it was good enough for my feet. Still, at the end of each day, my feet would start throbbing from the pounding, aided by the extra weight of my gear, but that didn't matter because my emotional drive to walk was greater than the physical pain telling me to stop.

COMBAT HAS NO EFFECT

A few days down the trail, I stopped in town for another zero-day and met two Veterans of the sandbox wars having dinner at the bar. They told me through whiskey-soaked breath that being in combat had had no effect on them. I talked about getting legislation passed; their rebuttal was simply, "civilians are assholes."

I agreed with them to an extent, but also saw it could be a case of ignorance. Civilians did not know what Service members went through. This observation was not received well by my dinner companions. I noticed a sudden shift in mood as their body language changed. They stiffened up, as sharks do when you encroach on their territory and arched their backs. Their movements slowed and became more deliberate. I knew they could explode in an instant. Never losing eye contact, their narrowing focus became needle point. With raised shoulders, their voices took on a flesh-cutting edge. When my dinner arrived, they continued attempting to drown out the past while I ate under their gaze, which screamed of threats and fears. Nevertheless, the conversation was defused and the topic wasn't broached again.

On the walk out of town, a Vietnam Combat Veteran approached me as if he was still on active duty: on guard, wary, and keeping a safe distance. "When I was there, I would do whatever it took to come home, but I was angry when I returned. But after finding the Lord seven years ago, now I have peace." He asked what I had to protect myself from bears on the trail.

"Nothing, I'm not afraid."

"I carry a .45; I'm not afraid either." Days after we parted, he contacted me to tell me he realized he was afraid.

The best way to tell me I'm wrong is to let me figure it out myself. The best way to tell me another way is to show me.

AA AND ACOA

After listening to his confession, a memory flashed through my mind: the first of only three Alcoholics Anonymous (AA) meetings I had gone to in my life. My family said I had a drinking problem and they incessantly nagged me, begging me to go to AA, which I finally did just to shut them up. At my first meeting, the woman sitting next to me said, "You're afraid."

"I am not afraid!" I yelled back at her. (Years later, I realized I was—why else would I have screamed at a little old lady?)

At the second meeting, they told me, "You'll be in these rooms with us for the rest of your life."

I said, "I'd rather drink than be with you clowns," and left. I became (what they call in the AA world) a dry drunk.

I went to the third meeting 30 years later while walking across the US. I only attended to support a friend who asked me to share my story.

I'm not saying AA doesn't work; that route just didn't work for me. I also went to Adult Children of Alcoholics (ACOA) because of the constant nagging of my sister, Denise. During those few meetings with her, I would interrupt and make fun of her till she burst into tears.

I sat there thinking, "What have I done? How could I hurt one of the few people who loves me enough to subject herself to this abuse?" That moment, I realized I had a problem and I stayed in ACOA for one and a half years, continuing to blame my parents till I realized it was me. Later, I sought counseling, but I never brought everything up because I wasn't even aware of the "stuff" I still held onto. That "stuff" didn't emerge until I did the walks and wrote this book.

THE LUCKY B&B

One day, I walked 18 miles to a trailhead (where the trail meets a road) and had another four miles to go to a rendezvous location with my second ex-wife at a B&B. By the time I reached the trailhead, I was already beat and figured I'd hitch a ride the rest of the way.

A truck stopped to ask me what I was doing. After explaining, I asked for a ride. "We don't have room." The back of the truck was empty and there were only two of them in the cab. I thought they were kidding until they sped away laughing.

I was pissed and, by the time I reached the B&B (a historic mansion), my feet were screaming and my soles were fried from walking the extra four miles on blacktop that had been baking in the day's 90-degree temperatures. When I went to register, the desk clerk said, "That will be $186.50."

"Where's the next closest one?"

She smiled and said, "Five miles away and it's the same price. We love hikers."

"Yeah, really?"

"Meals are included."

Once I was checked into my room, I took three showers, left all the lights and the TV on, ate the tooth paste and went to dinner. I ate as much as they would serve me, which wasn't much (there must have been some disaster, the way the food was rationed). While eating, I told the lady next to me why I was hiking.

"I have to introduce you to my husband. He writes for a paper with a circulation of 250,000 readers."

The next day, I met with her husband. We talked and he said, "I have to hook you up with Jim McDermott—a congressman from Washington State." A few days later, Jim McDermott's office called to set up an informal hearing three months out in September 2007. Full of excitement, I called my brother to tell him the news.

"Don't go. It's a trap."

My brother and I had done questionable things—things that would earn politicians a disappointed head shake for youthful follies but would earn us jail time. My brother's sense of humor gave me a moment's pause.

Knowing that my prior issues with the South Hampton authorities could catch up with me at any time, I thought he could be right. Then I realized, "What do the feds care about some guy fighting with the town? Boy, I've been in the woods too long."

What were the odds of meeting that writer? If my feet weren't that sore, I never would've paid $186.50 for that room, and I never would've made that connection. From then on, I made it a point to stop in towns along the way to increase exposure of my mission through the press. It was then that I felt everything was working perfectly.

***

What were the odds of meeting that writer?

THIRSTY JOE

I came upon a man wearing (what I thought were) two five-pound fire extinguishers strapped to his chest. His trail name was Thirsty Joe and he knew a lot about PTSD. "It's a traumatic experience changing your neurological hardware. It's a survival thing. At night, your brain will process this data unless you are in a fight or flight mode. Then it will store it and process it at a later date. If you're having trouble processing it or not having deep sleep to allow for processing, it becomes a nightmare. And when you can't deal with it, it becomes a disorder."

I asked about the two large canisters strapped to his chest and he explained that it was repellent for black bears and dogs, which may explain why he knew so much about PTSD. Joe believed in his repellent system so much he didn't give attacks a second thought; he was at peace.

Thirsty Joe's setup made me think of the difference between black and brown bear scat. Black bear scat has berries and seeds in it while brown has bits of plastic, metal, clothing, traces of mace, and meat.

There could be a positive aspect of PTSD: realizing you're human—furniture and rocks don't have PTSD. Furniture doesn't tremble every time it sees a fat lady about to sit on it, and a rock doesn't shake when it sees a sledgehammer.

I began to realize that beliefs don't have to be true, but they do make you stop searching for the truth as if you've found it already. A belief can also make you think that anyone with a different point of view is wrong. What if everything I believed was wrong?

INTEL

I was picked up at a trailhead to speak at a little church in Lancaster, Pennsylvania. This was arranged by a few women I met on Mount Washington. After I spoke, a man in his mid-twenties asked to talk with me privately. He was in counterintelligence for the military and applied that experience to the private sector after being discharged. When we sat down behind closed doors, he cried from a sea of blue eyes on which sorrow sailed.

After a moment of silence, he said, "Finally, someone I can talk to who understands the burden I carry. They told me if there was any possibility of weapons of mass destruction, say they exist—even if there is no proof. I followed orders from people in the defense-contracting business who didn't consider themselves mercenaries, but corporate patriots leading from the rear. Now my friends are dead because of my intel. What can I do?"

Coincidentally, at the shelter the night before, Solitaire and Stretch told me a story about Gandhi (my favorite skinhead for peace). He and his son went into town to get the car fixed and the son wanted to go to the movies. Gandhi said, "Check back at 4 pm."

The son said, "Okay," and went to the theater.

At four, Gandhi went back to the car, but the son didn't show, having decided to stay for the double feature. At six, the son arrived, and Gandhi asked, "Were you here at 4 pm?"

"Yes, but the car wasn't done."

Gandhi said nothing. The boy hopped in the driver's seat to head home and asked his dad to get in. Gandhi refused. "I will walk the six miles." When the son asked why, he said, "I want to contemplate what I've done that would cause you to lie to me." His son drove by his side the whole way home and never lied again.

The young man from Lancaster drove the same car.

CAPTAIN MIKE

Meeting that young man took me back to my high school graduation and my first full-time job in the Merchant Marines working on a tramp steamer, emulating a man called Captain Mike.

At the age of eleven, in my constant quest to stay away from home, I worked on a party boat for a man named Captain Mike Shinuta, supposedly of Polish royalty. He sailed the seas with Frank Buck on a tramp steamer, sleeping in a hammock over a panda bear in cargo. It was a time when sailing out to sea was a method of escaping your past to start a new life.

Having never heard him curse or yell (or speak above a whisper, for that matter), he became my idol; I watched every move he made. One day, he walked up to a group of rowdy, loud, cursing bikers. He said a few quiet words, and they slowed down, lowered their voices, and left.

Later I asked, "How come you don't curse or talk loud like the others?"

"I don't have to in order to get my point across," he said quietly.

That was who I wanted to be.

In my attempt to emulate Captain Mike, I got a job on a freighter and traveled halfway around the world to India, Africa, Pakistan, and Arabia delivering military equipment. This was after the US signed a peace treaty with Israel, so I asked, "How can we sell weapons to the enemies of our friends?"

My shipmates laughed and said, "It's all about money."

Before that day, I had lived in a black-and-white world, where I held everybody to the standard to which they held me. At that moment, though, I saw gray. It shook my belief in the history I'd been taught— how America always did the right thing. Everything was in question. It seemed that, just a few weeks prior, I was riding around town on my bike, reading comics and debating whether Santa came down the chimney.

Before I was told, "It's all about money," my life had been sheltered from a world I knew nothing about. How was I to navigate through it with a broken moral compass? How would I deal with the consequences of my actions if I were to hold myself to the standards I held everyone else? I felt off course. Had I just done what billions before me had done? Would I justify the things I would do with half-truths and denials?

Wrestling with this conflict, I wondered if there was a way I'd ever make it to Catholic heaven, reasoning that my best chance was to die immediately because the longer I lived, the more chance there was that I would sin and go to hell. If I killed myself to avoid that, though, I believed I would go to hell anyway.

Staring into the abyss between right and wrong, heaven and hell, it seemed there was no hope unless there was a loophole. From my understanding, God forgave people who atoned for their sins. At that point in my life, I hadn't been sorry enough to change my behaviors, so long as I could crawl to the confessional before the lights went out.

Part of my job, as an ordinary seaman, was to stand watch for two hours every night on the bow of the ship. The first night, I asked myself, "Why am I here? What is the point?" After standing alone every night for two months, staring into the dark, my mind went blank. I had a sense of stillness and a sensation that I wasn't a body, but a warm golden light that encompassed everything; there was nothing else.

I understood that humans are here to love one another; that's what it was all about. I was fearless, at peace with the world and all its components. I saw love as an energy that made up everything—an energy that couldn't be destroyed. Why kill myself out of worry about going to hell when God is love and there's nothing else?

My words pale to this experience, but it's the best I can do to convey my thoughts and feelings of those moments. I understood everything was an experience and there was a need to be present in each moment of each experience, without getting attached and adding things to it that aren't there. I started to live without guilt or internal judgment—simply being and enjoying the moment.

After coming back from sea and hitting the states, I wanted to experience what it was like to live as an apostle. So, I went on the road with five dollars and the clothes on my back. I had a month before I was needed back on the ship, so I headed to Kansas to meet a pen pal. While on my journey, people said to me, "There is something about you I want." I took that state of bliss for granted, but later learned it needed to be nourished if it was to be maintained (it was buried in the Marine Corps).

I decided to buy a mountain and live my new lifestyle. I told Stuart, who I met in Memphis on my way back from Kansas, about my plans. He became my first apostle, a friend that believes in you and your cause. Life, however, had another path in mind for me—one unaffected by my desires. I wouldn't be able to enjoy my new lifestyle for long.

I used the $3,500 I had saved while at sea in 1968 to buy 156 acres with a cabin and electricity in Franklin County (upstate New York). The cabin was a two-story structure with tarpaper roofing for siding, a potbelly stove for heat, a wood-burning stove for cooking, a pitcher pump for water, and a toilet in the closet (later replaced by an outhouse).

The first time up, I passed the cabin (located on a dirt road off a dirt road) because it was hidden by the growth. Nonetheless, it was mine. There, I'd be free to live out the life I'd envisioned while at sea—a fairytale where I believed I would live happily ever after. I was there for an entire summer before enlisting in the USMC. I let Stuart and whoever he invited (and whoever they invited) stay there, so it eventually became a commune (that, or simply a lot of guests in an anarchist household).

While I was still there, the people that came asked me, "What do you want me to do?"

I replied, "Just be."

Looking back, it was like having a garden that you didn't weed, expecting that the fruits and flowers you wanted would flourish on their own. Weeding would have been discipline; water and fertilizer would have been education. Some commune devotees walked away, shaking their heads, not knowing where to release all the baggage they had brought with them, finding it even harder to release after they had found someone with matching luggage.

I remember thinking, "Now we can do what we want. We're out of parents' house." I didn't realize that most of us were so well-programmed that our behaviors hadn't changed —just our location.

When I left, I provided no plan or rules to help the others gain the insight and experience I had, expecting they would find it on their own by sitting and starring into the darkness. What was I thinking? There were a few whose luggage matched my own (Barry Schulz, Stuart Abraham, Beau Ives, and Dale Tuzzeo) and, even though we exchanged some luggage, our friendships transcended time.

We had young people from all walks of life on the property: members of Timothy Leary's Church and Hog Farm, Buddhists, born-again spiritualists, drug dealers, and local kids wanting to be rebellious hippies. We were disillusioned with the world we thought our parents had made, not realizing they were born and programmed into it just like us.

Going back into the woods after getting discharged from the USMC, I understood their frustration with my response, "Just be." I was unable to understand or act upon it myself.

I had lost my way again, after being immersed in a world of hate, extreme prejudice, and fear. I became like so many that had come to me, hoping that just a geographical change would transform something intangible inside me, without having to discipline my mind.

SERIAL KILLER

I met Caveman in a hostel in Delaware. We spent the night talking, and he told me to look up his family when I got to Boiling Springs, PA. Papa Caveman was in public relations for the police and told me he had been invited to a seminar given by the FBI about serial killers. The FBI conducted an in-depth study to find out what makes them tick, using that information to apprehend others.

One serial killer they studied had been the subject of an FBI movie. When he was a child, his father took him to bars but left him in the car. Later in the night, his father would bring a woman into the car and rape her while his son was still there. When he turned 12, his father let him rape them when he was finished. When he was caught as an adult and interviewed for trapping women in his house before killing them, he said, "The way my father did it seemed inefficient. So, I would keep them till I got tired of them—then kill them."

Papa Caveman said, "In the beginning, I couldn't even conceive of these things. But after hearing the childhood stories, I saw how he could make that leap to where he is now."

Parents (sometimes unknowingly) build a foundation for their children by how they carry themselves—that foundation remains under construction into their early twenties. What foundation had I and my peers been built upon? How did the trauma of war test that foundation? Being was the blocks themselves, action was the mortar, and words were the stucco. How far did I deviate from the blueprint my father had given me?

WASHINGTON, DC

September 26th at Front Royal, I took a zero-day to shave and wash my clothes (by taking a shower in them and giving them a final rinse in the sink, watching the dirt flow down the drain). I was hoping to look and smell fairly human, thus making it easier for my "peeps" (my sister and her friends) to ride in the car with me with the windows up as we traveled to Washington, DC for my informal hearing.

Once in DC, I met with Congressman McDermott's PR man, who told me what to expect and matched names to faces. He explained that security was crazy, since some guy got deep into the White House with a gun, creating checkpoints in the tunnels that ran underneath. He told me to meet him at the office by nine in the morning, not to worry (he repeated this several times), not to be intimidated, and to show up the way I walked the trail (barefoot, wrapped in my homemade paper gear and wearing the same clothes I had worn for months). I told him not to worry—that I was fine and hoped he wouldn't be offended that I had washed and cleaned my clothes.

"I believe things work out for the best."

He said, "I believe you have to work at it."

Transitioning from seeing a few people a day that left a tiny footprint on the earth to walking on a surface that man crushed into submission with mountains of concrete and steel, hiding the earth from the sun with tar and infesting it with humans (the equivalent of the locust and termites of nature) was surreal. Roaming those streets, I imagined power brokers meeting to decide the fate of the world, while self-serving people laid in ambush to catch one of them in a moment of weakness.

On the day of the hearing, going through security, I had to part with my walking sticks because they were potential weapons. Continuing to the conference room, everything was fine until I came around the corner and saw a bare oak table with three microphones in the center. Suddenly, I was a man in the trunk of a car going to an undisclosed location to dig his own grave. My feet started to sweat. So much for not worrying.

I calmed myself down the best I could by trying to put things into context (not as easy as it sounds). I mingled, listened, and talked to those that came up to me. People told me it was an honor to meet me, which took me by surprise. I hadn't thought walking barefoot in tattered clothes garnished with Tyvek did much compared to actions of politicians, department heads, and organizations—not because they happened to dress and smell better than me, but because they were in positions of power. I realize now that it wasn't about that power, but about finding a way to capture the public's imagination and attention.

At the head table was Max Cleland, a former senator from Georgia, the congressman from Maine, Michael Michaud (the head of Veterans Affairs), and Jim McDermott. John Kerry had endorsed the event but was unable to attend.

Jim spoke first, then Max, both dubbing PTSD as a topic that needed to be addressed and recognizing the men in attendance who would do something about it. I felt intimidated because Max Cleland lost three limbs to save his buddies in the Army, while I was someone that stood up for my beliefs by refusing to go to war, and could have lost my life or freedom stateside.

I had prayed while in the woods and at the hotel, "God, help me speak when I get there. If I show up without you, it's going to be a mess." When it was my turn to speak, I was wound up so tight that I couldn't even sit—so I stood. I spoke from my heart about being prepared to go to prison or face a firing squad for my beliefs and about my experiences, both during and after, with the Marines that drove me to walk.

Congressman Mike spoke and said, "How can I follow what Ron said?" (He did anyway.) Garrett, representing Iran and Afghanistan Veterans of America (IAVA), said a few words. Then Patrick, another Veteran who walked the halls of Washington, talked about how he held his buddy's head in his lap, trying to hold his brains in as he died.

After we were done, Max embraced me. Tears fell from his eyes as he said, "Welcome home. You're doing more than me."

That blew me away. Who was I compared to a senator with access to all the tools that (I thought) could help our troops? An older gentleman shook my hand and said, "Keep up the good work."

Next was a news conference. I sat at the front table with Max and Jim. Jim introduced me, and a reporter asked me a question. I started talking and got worked up, raising my voice, explaining that soldiers want to be the heroes that end war. Jim squeezed my leg (maybe it was political, or maybe he just liked me), so I brought it down a notch. Max spoke, and then it was over. I mingled as much as a toe mingles with fingers, went over to the older gentleman, and said, "You shook my hand earlier. Who are you?"

"I was Jim McDermott's commanding officer, like a father to him. You were the type of person I wouldn't have liked, but I understand now. You taught me something. Thank you."

I asked how old he was, and he said he was 81. I told him that my father was 80, and he said, "I am your father." I don't think he meant it in a Darth Vader sort of way.

One of Jim's aides guided me to the cafeteria to meet my sister and friends, but they were missing in action. I waited in Jim's office while search parties were sent out and calls were made with no response.

At his office, I got a glimpse of who he was: the last line of defense for the underdog. It was nice to see there were people in Washington like that; it gave me hope.

My sister and friends finally arrived, after having had tea with a senator they met. No wonder the search party couldn't find them—they were hiding in plain sight. We said our goodbyes.

A few hours later, back at the trailhead, we had a short healing ceremony, during which everybody knelt and placed their hands on me as I laid flat on my back. Cars stopped and people asked if they could help.

Finally, I was released back into the wild. After trekking far enough into the woods to drown out the sights and sounds of traffic, I sat down to contemplate the great things our leaders said that made me feel warm and fuzzy—and what all those great things meant. *Was it just hot air up my shorts? Would something get done? How would they do it?*

It was a radical transition, going from being the center of attention at the capitol to sitting alone off the grid, thinking my job was almost done. I just had to finish the walk.

I would find later it was just beginning.

"You were the type of person I wouldn't have liked,
but I understand now."

THUNDER AND LIGHTING

A few hours after my return to the woods, with nothing but the sound of crickets, I crossed paths with Druid on the way to Priest Shelter. He looked like someone ran over his dog. He had recently broken up with his girlfriend because her brother, who had just returned from Iraq and was unable to care for himself, had moved in with her. It was as if the stork just dropped off a basket, destroying their relationship, and he was there "to search for answers."

Shortly after we parted ways, it got dark and foggy. In mere seconds, the wind went from zero to skinning the ground, and the sky opened up to crush the earth under rain, thunder, and lightning. I was bounced off the ground by a bolt about 50 feet away and I could barely see. Thank God I was just in sight of the shelter before the blinding rain; otherwise, I would have walked right by it.

The first time I remember hearing thunder, I was four and awakened in the middle of the night, scared by a bolt of lightning that split the sky and shook the house. My father came into my room and asked, "What's the matter?"

"I'm afraid."

"There's nothing to be afraid of. It's God's fireworks." He touched me on the shoulder and held me close to calm my fears. Pointing to a lightning bolt, he said, "Oh look at that one! Isn't it pretty?" Seeing him smile in the flashes, I gazed at him in wonder and went back to sleep, safe and sound while God continued his show.

EXTENDED ZERO DAYS

My back pain had been getting worse for several months. Even taking extended zero-days didn't seem to help because my legs went numb. With no improvement, I agonized about what to do and finally decided to get off the trail and heal. It was one of the hardest things I had done. I felt like I was letting everyone down, including myself. I also knew, if something didn't change, there was no way I could finish.

Making my final decision, I called one of the people with whom I had been in frequent contact since starting an email exchange early in the walk. The man's son, a practicing Buddhist with a genius-level IQ, had locked himself in his room for a year after returning from combat. At the end of that year, he completed suicide, leaving his parents in despair. They later divorced. I asked him to forgive me for having to interrupt my mission.

He said he was glad I was taking care of myself, and we were able to meet at the end of the trail with Max Cleland for an event my son and I had planned in order to create more awareness.

Allowing myself time to heal, I hung in a homemade traction rack because the main contributor to the problem was all the weight from the backpack on my shoulders, com-pressing my spine with constant pressure on my nerves. My sister (a seamstress) and I remade the gear. In minutes, she was able to shift the load to the hips, something that would have taken me hours to do.

It was one of the hardest things I had done.

BACK ON THE TRAIL

After five months of being in an alternate universe of spine decompression and civilization, my girlfriend Jill drove me from Long Island to the B&B Dutch Haus in Montebello. The date was April 15, 2007.

With my reconstructed backpack, which I didn't overload (for a change), I picked up where I left off, doing an easy eight-mile day, (four out and four back) and spent another night at the B&B. I felt great—no pain.

While Jill was down for the count, I celebrated by going to a poker game with the B&B owner and some locals. Three were Veterans with issues—two had trouble holding a steady job. I fit right in and was wholeheartedly accepted, as I single-handedly helped the local economy with my generous donation at the table that night.

One happy recipient, an optometrist, had been recently asked by the VA to check the eyesight of those coming back from the service.

"The concussions from the improvised explosive devices," he said, "are so severe that they affect their eyesight, but that is the least of their worries because their brains are scrambled by the explosions. Right now [2007], the VA is so understaffed that the same 30 people were still sitting in the lobby when I left two hours later."

He hadn't been called back, so he didn't know what the VA ended up doing.

I fit right in and was wholeheartedly accepted

TRAIL LORE

Who had it better than me? I put in an easy 15 miles, aided by gentle slopes and stone-less dirt with a carpet of pine needles, to arrive at a shelter, greeted by Mouse Trap, Pilgrim, Angel, some day-hikers, and a local. Tales were told of a woman, who said she was a queen, staying at the shelter. The park rangers asked her to leave because she had filled it with trash. "We're not sure who she really is," the local said, but it didn't matter what her title was—the trail had a way of striping away a person's disguise.

There was another tale of a hiker who called himself Saved. He hiked at night with a dog and went up to people's tents, shining his light in and saying, "You're going to die," to some and, "You're going to live," to others.

"He was really freaking people out." No kidding. Saved changed his trail name to evade the rangers who wanted to throw him off the trail, but the only description they had, because he hiked at night, was that he might wear glasses and have a red beard. Listening to the story, I glanced through my spectacles down at my reddish beard.

I loved those trail tales. Wouldn't it be great if all we had to do to enact our transformation was change our name or move to a different town? When people are on the trail for a few months, it's not the trail that changes them—it's simply a place that allows them to change. On the trail, you get great counseling: your own.

———◆•◈•◆———

The trail had a way of striping away a person's disguise.

FOOD FOR THOUGHT

Before leaving town, where I spent a zero-day and talked to a newspaper reporter in Pearisburg (134'elv.), I went to Hardee's for breakfast. I usually never eat in places like that, being that my body is a temple—a temple of doom, that is.

After placing my order, I told the cashier what I was doing. She said, "I have PTSD because my house burned down, and my boss is stressed because his son is in Iraq."

While I waited for my order, the guy next to me, a correctional officer, said, "My daughter is a wreck because one of her friends died at the Virginia Tech shooting. Some Vets I've dealt with have shot themselves or their spouses and themselves. Something should be done to help prevent it."

I was surprised, finding myself in a generic fast-food joint, seeing this small crosscut of rural America. On the surface, everything looked normal (whatever that is), but underneath, everything was a mess—paint coating a rotting piece of wood. Each one of those people thought they were alone in their suffering, held it in, and didn't talk about it, letting it fester instead of heal—and yet they also each thought it was something someone else should fix.

Leaving Hardee's, I got to the Partnership Shelter in what seemed like a short time, as my mind had been wandering. At the shelter, I met Fireball, a Marine home on leave, hiking with his future wife. We talked about PTSD, which he said he had, and his decision not to ship back out to be with his buddies. He said his buddies were the only reason he even considered going back; it had nothing to do with why they were there.

Being close enough to a town and the main highway, we ordered out for food using one of my co-hiker's cellphone. The restaurant took advantage of us by overcharging for the food, charging for delivery, and demanding a tip once the food got there. When I was in business, seeing people as merely an opportunity for monetary gain, how far would I have gone for millions? The other end of the stick didn't feel so good.

Turns out that delivery meal came with a hearty dose of contemplation.

THE ROAD TO DAMASCUS

When I walked part of the Appalachian Trail in 1998, I arrived in Damascus, Virginia in time for "Trail Days" (an annual week-long reunion of thousands of hikers). It was like being back in the '60s.

There was a live radio broadcast of interviews conducted in the parking lot of a gas station and other events throughout town, including a variety of onstage performances by hikers in the town park.

I was introduced to Earl Shaffer, a soft-spoken man who was the first to walk the entire Appalachian Trail (50 years prior). He was an Army Veteran from WWII who, walking 17 miles a day, completed the hike from Mt. Oglethorpe, Georgia to Mt. Katahdin, Maine in 1948. It was no small feat and rumor had it, he slept standing up next to trees.

When I met him in 1998, he was in the process of repeating the hike at 79 years old.

On the surface, everything looked normal (whatever that is), but underneath, everything was a mess ...

FLASHBACK

More than a decade later, I found myself once again in Damascus in time for Trail Days. This time, Vets were coming up to me shaking my hand. One hiker told me he came from Key Largo, Florida to meet me because he had heard I would be there. It was a blast being surrounded by so many like-minded people and being treated like a legend, as I was the second person to walk the trail barefoot (supposedly, some guy from South Africa had done it years before, but I think he was lying). We ate like we were going into hibernation, talked about gear with manufacturers, and were given free accessories.

The best part was meeting so many hikers I had heard about through the trail grapevine. I was able to put faces to names and share stories that only other hikers could appreciate: why we were hiking, what we learned, and what our philo-sophies were. Best of all, we were able to support one another in our quests.

While there, I met with Penny Coleman, a writer who would walk part of the trail with me upon departure. She wrote "Flashback" (her trail name), a story about Vietnam's effect on her and her husband, who had died by suicide. It was an honor to meet her and prepare for our little stroll at Crazy Larry's Hostel (Larry's personal home that he opened up to hikers).

She was concerned about the weight of her pack and her ability to manage the walk. Some preparation was necessary before we left, which meant reducing the weight of her pack by taking out all her extra clothes and store-bought gear. Just because it looked good in the catalog didn't mean it was necessary. Who needs a tent when they have shelters, or a heavy metal canteen when you can use a plastic bottle that weighs an ounce? There is no point at which you can be totally prepared. You just have to pull the trigger and accept the consequences of what the hike will bring.

Before Penny and I left for the trail, we met Sergeant Rock, a First Sergeant in the Army who was involved in troop deployment to Afghanistan and Iraq. He had just returned to the States days before. He taught me that Blackwater and other defense contractors recruit people for support, such as truck drivers, firemen, cooks—all the way up to mercenaries. It reinforced what I heard from others about how many salaried non-military personnel provided support services. It allows the government to underreport the number of soldiers in an area of conflict.

How do you regulate non-military personnel in a war zone? What laws do they fall under?

Sergeant Rock also told us about the mentality of the Iraqis. "They think you don't like them if you order them around. That means they don't follow orders the way you mean them, so you end up having to reprimand them." He gave an example of some Iraqi soldiers who didn't show up for work for a few days. When they came back, they were asked, "Where have you been? You didn't show up for work."

They said, "I was at work. I was protecting my home and neighborhood," and expected to be paid.

It reminded me of a woman on welfare that had six children. The agency told her she had to get a job.

"What about my children?"

"We will hire someone to watch them," which would cost approximately the same amount of money she would receive with a job. It didn't make sense to me.

Who would do a better job of taking care of her children than her? On the other hand, what are our systems (both mil-itary and domestic) doing to perpetuate this mess by ignoring the source of the problems? I hope someday we become more inventive and create jobs that make our world better by creating long-term solutions instead of short-term fixes.

Sergeant Rock continued to educate us. "The troops will go in, secure an area, leave, come back in six months, and find it was like they had never been there. When the troops leave, they go back to a tactically secure area, a base surrounded by barb wire, leaving the people without a continuing, functional security force."

He also told us that most of the people leading troops from the rear were politicians, with no military experience, trying to run the war like a business.

I guess it is. Even if you have the experience, there's a time-lapse and mistranslation from the ground to the office that cripples the effort. It's hard to restock the ammo shelf when you're in a firefight, and the guy giving the approval for delivery is thousands of miles away speaking Greek instead of military jargon, trying to save 50 cents.

Perhaps we should contract out political positions in DC and pay by performance. It would probably be more cost-effective.

Once Penny and I were on the trail, we spent every night in a shelter and (wouldn't you know it) it didn't rain once. One night, she grabbed my leg, waking me up. When I had my wits about me, I thought to myself, *Thank you, God! Tonight is my lucky night.* Out loud I said, "What?"

Before she answered in those brief nanoseconds, it was obvious to me that she could no longer resist me and wanted me sexually, due to our bonding on the trail and my undeniable animal charisma. (I think all women want me—when I was drunk, I knew they did.) What did it matter that she was gay? I assumed she was crossing over that night.

"You're snoring," she said. Needless to say, I was baffled but went back to sleep.

The next morning, I told her what I thought when she grabbed my leg. She laughed and said, "Oh, I have touched the hem of history."

———◆•◆•◆———

Perhaps we should contract out political positions in DC and pay by performance.

JAPANESE DOCUMENTARY

I met Yoshidfumi, Shibako, Teesuo Sato, and Yoshihiro Shiroki from NHK (Japanese Public Broadcast), who happened to be driving by when Flashback and I got to a trail-head. They stopped, backed up, and asked me if I had seen Tyvek.

Looking down at my feet to make sure, I confirmed, "Yeah, I'm him."

They wanted me to be part of a documentary they intended to shoot about the healing effects of the Appalachian Trail, but they had to get permits from our government first. I thought it would be ironic if I ended up being better known in Japan than here.

They did a short interview to show their people back home, took us to lunch, dropped me off at the hostel, and took Flashback back to her car.

When she left, I felt a tinge of loneliness after sharing time with someone on a similar path, even though she was able to resist my baby cobalt blues.

I thought it would be ironic if I ended up being
better known in Japan than here.

THE RAIN

Rounding a bend in the trail, I came upon First Sergeant, a Special Forces retiree, sitting on the ground against a tree. "I wish I'd been told what signs to look for when I got out," he began after we chatted for a bit. "It would have been easier on my family. When I got out, I was invited to talk at Gold Star Mothers functions but had to stop because I would start crying for no reason. I went for counseling to find out why. I put my family, especially my wife through hell."

His tone reflected a tinge of regret coupled with resig-nation, "I love when it rains. I could sit all day in the rain. When it rained in deployment, we weren't trying to kill one another."

One therapist I had met from Miami, Dr. Albert Zbik, gave a lecture at Mariners Hospital, and he described PTSD as your mind being separated into bins, with different experiences filling up each bin. After one got full and you encountered another event that would fall into that bin, it would cause a traumatic reaction.

I cry when I see the "Little Mermaid." Her father gave his life for hers.

———◆•◆•◆———

I cry when I see the "Little Mermaid."
Her father gave his life for hers.

GIARDIA

One area I stopped in contained a blight that had killed thousands of trees. On top of that, there was no water, and I had run dry. A couple told me there was water off a blue trail and they would get some for me. When they brought it back, they warned that it was dirty.

I thanked them and bragged, "That's okay. I haven't been purifying my water. I drank from a mud puddle once and was fine." So, when they gave me the bottle, I took a swig without looking.

There are moments when action and regret are near-simultaneous—much like this one. The taste was bitter and I could feel the gunk in it as it slide (crawled?) down my throat. When I looked, I saw floating mouse turds and mosquito larva.

I got giardia. It was coming out both ends: vomit out the top and severe Hershey squirts out the bottom. I was getting weaker by the day, unable to hold anything down. Three days later, I made it to a town and purchased some black walnut extract at a health food store to stop the loss. I was already 20 pounds lighter.

Another lesson in humility that I failed: people say what doesn't kill you makes you stronger.

I say it just makes you sick.

There are moments when action and
regret are near simultaneous ...

THE BOMB

At nine in the morning, the day before I was set to arrive at Springer Mountain (the endpoint of my Appalachian Trail hike), the Japanese filmmakers arrived at the shelter I'd slept at, having obtained permission to film the documentary. Also staying at the shelter was a family unit: a mother, a father, and two children. It was encouraging to see a healthy, wholesome family pursuing such a hike together, and I feel nostalgic for when my two boys were little.

Once the film crew and I parted ways with the family, we hiked the three and a half miles to Three Forks. We talked, and the crew got footage of me speaking with other hikers. We backtracked by van to Neil's Gap so they could photograph me in a hostel, and we spent the night. While I was talking with the patrons, one couple looked at me funny until they realized who I was. The woman said, "I read about you."

"Did you write to your Congressman?"

"No."

I said, "Stick out your hand," which she did. I playfully smacked it and asked, "Now are you going to write?"

"Yes," she said.

"Good. I don't want to have to do this again."

The following day, we backtracked to Three Forks and walked the remainder of the way to Springer Mountain. Caught in a downpour, the whole crew got soaked except me (I was prepared with my Tyvek outfit and matching accouterments). Once I arrived at Springer Mountain, I screamed for joy, kissed the marker officially designating the ending point of the 2,174 mile Appalachian Trail, wrote my name in the registry, then knelt and thanked God for my safe arrival. I made so much noise screaming for joy that a hiker named Mandolin came running from the shelter to see who was hurt.

My year of nights sleeping on the trail, insulated from the ground or the wood floor of a three-sided shelter by a piece of Tyvek paper and a piece of felt, was about to end. I had come to find the ground was a soft mattress after 16-hour days of kicking rocks and roots that had done nothing to deserve my assault. I began to feel nostalgic for each bit of my year-long mission as I contemplated the people I had talked with, the hands I had held, and the hugs I had shared.

I was filmed going to sleep, brushing my teeth—everything but relieving myself (I think). Most of the shots would end up on the cutting room floor. What they did keep was some film of me bathing naked in a stream and hugging a tree. (It's officially documented: I am a tree-hugging AT porn star.) My Japanese friends and I sat for hours around the campfire that last night, trying (with little luck) to keep it going despite the hard rain.

We were still damp when we awoke the following morning and made the drive into Dahlonega, where the crew filmed me walking into town. Along the way, there were white crosses planted every 20 yards, each engraved with the name of a serviceman and the war in which they died. After filming that last walk, the Japanese film crew asked me how I felt.

"Sad and angry—sad that they died and angry that we honor the dead with lip service instead of taking care of the living they left behind."

When I'm dead, you can run me through a woodchipper and use me for chum, but please take care of those I left behind. It's embarrassing to know that we have so much time on our hands that we put effort into having a "National Ice Cream Day." Don't get me wrong, I love ice cream, but wouldn't it be more productive to spend our time and energy instituting laws and programs that change people's lives for the better, especially the lives of our Veterans, many of whom have sacrificed so much, both in war and its aftermath?

When we were done with the documentary, I asked the crew, "Why?"

They responded, "Because you are the only country to use an atomic bomb and we are the only country to receive it. We want to know what you are thinking."

"Because you are the only country
to use an atomic bomb and we are the only country
to receive it. We want to know what you are thinking."

MEDIA EVENT

My son Zachariah and I set up a media event at the end of my hike. On the 4th of July 2007, we had a band and actors performing two shows at a hall we rented (we had spent over $10,000). We gave out 200 free tickets.

I was to speak at the event, along with Michael Duckett (the father who lost his son, a five-time decorated Green Beret, to suicide—the man from whom I had asked forgiveness when I interrupted my hike and mission to heal my back) We also invite the former Georgia Senator Max Cleland, who I had last seen in Washington, DC.

Fifteen people showed up for the event, most of whom were my family members. When I went on stage and saw so few in attendance, an old thought pattern, from when I had gotten out of the Marines, reemerged. *So what? Who cares? In the end, it doesn't matter.*

Upon further consideration, though, I thought, *It matters to those few out there and it matters to us*, so we carried on to those few who filled the house. How arrogant of me to believe that whatever I did didn't matter—that no one cared.

Everything matters, and I care!

My son and I understood that each one of those people was important. We also realized that we needed to learn how to better promote an event.

———◆·◆·◆———

It matters to those few out there and it matters to us

THE KEYS

Just before I finished my hike, my youngest sister Laurie told me that our dad had six months to live. After completing the event at the end of the trail, I dropped in on my father in Key Largo to see for myself. I stayed with him—how could I say that I support Veterans if I couldn't care for my own Veteran father?

He ended up living three more years. It seemed yelling at me during Pinochle was a rejuvenating exercise for him. If I'd known at the time, I would've thrown a few games.

Up to the time of his death, he would tell me, "I can still take you." There were many times in my life during which I would have liked to beat him, but now he was before me a wheelchair-dependent old man: blind, frail, and toothless, with a pacemaker, defibrillator, and diapers. What would I gain by kicking him now?

It was sad to see the man who had filled the screen of my life—with good, bad, and all the drama in between—reduced to a shadow of his former self. Watching him die, powerless to stop his suffering, I felt like a man trying to lift a weight he couldn't keep from dropping.

My father passed away on my mother's birthday, February 7th, a date I never remembered until then. I saw her heartbreak, as she wanted to die too. Her last few birthdays were sorrowful occasions. My father may have lasted longer, but he had come to feel he was too much of a burden for her and went into the hospital for an assessment to be placed in a VA home. That surprised me, as he had said he'd never go into a home. While being examined, he gave the nurses such a hard time that they sedated him to keep him quiet.

He never came out of it—never made it to the VA home. The only good thing about it was that God answered his prayer to end his suffering. In the last months of his life, the pace-maker constantly jumpstarted him, leaving him wishing he never had it. He sat in his wheelchair waiting to die with only two things still working: his mind and his mouth.

At the time surrounding my father's death, I was with Valeria, a woman I met at "A Course of Miracles" discussion group. She told me that she had personally struggled with PTSD. She said an absent father and a mother who was not forthcoming with factual information contributed to this.

The information she did have indicated that her father suffered greatly during his military service. She told me she had benefited from treatment—some of her symptoms lessened and others disappeared altogether. I later learned that most mental illnesses can be acerbated by stress.

While in Florida, I made a sandwich sign stating, "18 Vets a Day Commit SUICIDE! thelongwalkhome.org." I walked the length of the Keys wearing my sign and continued to carry the sign five days a week.

Three years after my second walk on the Appalachian Trail (a few weeks after my father passed), I was walking with my sign on a bright, cloudless Key Largo morning with the 95-degree heat bearing down on me. I began to feel that the sign wasn't creating enough awareness to get the desired legislation passed, so I decided to take it a step further by walking barefoot across the country.

I planned to use the opportunity to gather signatures for the petition I would later present in Washington, DC, after completing the cross-country journey. The petition asked for the implementation of the original three points I had conceived with Adam and Nicole Strauss.

1. Grieving classes during boot camp to provide an understanding of the five stages (denial, anger, bargaining, depression, and acceptance) that surface when someone su ers a loss so that they can identify what they're feeling;

2. Mandatory counseling prior to discharge to strip away the stigma of asking for help (more so than the usual debriefing); and

3. Available support groups after transitioning to civilian life (thankfully, there are currently many available through the VA).

I told Valeria about my plan to walk across the country. She said she would too, to help those with PTSD ... if we had a camper. She didn't think living in my beat-up Escort Station Wagon for almost a year would be sustainable (imagine that). I hoped she would join, as she was just as passionate about helping Veterans as I was, making her a partner in this effort.

VALERIA

We had a yard sale, selling nearly everything we owned to get money for the camper, gas, and food. We cut the lines to the dock, and whatever we hadn't sold was left behind, including our jobs and our Key Largo way of life.

Valeria gave up her support system to make my cause her own. Leaving the Florida Keys in a cloud of coral dust, our journey began, but it wouldn't be official until I started walking from Concord Mass (the chosen starting line of my barefoot hike across America).

Our first few hours on the road almost ended the venture. Valeria drove the camper like someone not wanting to die alone (as opposed to me, who drives like someone who doesn't want others to live). Not yet out of Florida, she hit the brakes particularly hard, causing the camper to veer to the right and the passenger-side mirror to collide with the back end of a tractor-trailer.

"Why are you screaming like a little girl?" she yelled at me. Having frightened both of us with her maneuver (and likely also frightened by the decibels of my response), she began to cry. She insisted that I drive, as she had never driven a camper before. That was fine for the moment, but what would we do when I started walking? Maybe I should have gotten the brakes adjusted before we left.

A few days later, she cried her way through a tunnel for what seemed like hours. I didn't know it was possible to cry for so long. I thought she would pass out from both dehydration and exhaustion. At the same time, I was getting ready to start my new adventure and rededicate myself to the mission to make a difference in the lives of returning Veterans; she was grieving the loss of her old life.

In retrospect, I realize how unsympathetic I was towards Valeria, another victim of the collateral damage of war. Living with her and the expectation that she would be totally focused on my goal, I was blind to who she was. I don't know if I could have done it without her (though I'd like to think I could have). I doubt that it would have been easier or more comfortable. She was a major contributor: driver, CFO, CEO, webpage master, greeter, listener of the people during many speaking engagements, and carrier of the emotional burden from those intense interactions.

FIRST STEPS ACROSS AMERICA: JUNE 1, 2010

We finally made it to Boston and stayed with Paulie, who had offered to let us use his house while in the area. I had met him at a party in Key Largo two years prior, his Boston-self and my New York-self bonding over our common sarcastic world view. He understood the weight of my mission because his brother had committed suicide.

I chose Concord, a town northwest of Boston as the starting point of my walk for its historical significance at the beginning of the Revolutionary War. All wars likely created soldiers with PTSD, despite the different names given, and the initial one to establish our nation's freedom was no different.

The first shot in the American Revolution was fired in Concord, so the story goes. The skirmish took place at North Bridge, where I stood to begin my walk. In 1775, farmers armed with whatever they had stood on one side, confronting trained British soldiers who eventually returned their volley of fire. In many of the good things we do, we do it until someone gets hurt; that's usually where it ends. At Concord's North Bridge, though, it did not end; rather, it began.

I imagined myself in place of those Minutemen called to action—fearful, with hopes of freedom, suffering conflicting thoughts of what could be gained or lost and whether it was worth pursuing. It was hard for me to conceive their state of mind—patriots standing up to what was then one of the most powerful armies in the world. I was attempting a stand against a lack of action from the country that was conceived by that "Shot heard around the world." My barefoot walk across America was the only way I knew to express my own brand of patriotism.

I took the first steps of my journey over that bridge, carrying the petition, wearing the sandwich sign. I would later modify my armor with Tyvek to make a pocket to hold petitions, add a hood, and create coverage on the sides to keep me drier and warmer, preventing rain from wicking off my heat. In my own beginning, my mission gave me purpose, as I employed my freedom of expression, for which those early Patriots had fought.

People asked, again, why I took this walk across America barefoot. There were a few reasons. First, I wasn't a big fan of shoes (except for safety), and not wearing shoes went against the norm. I'm a bit of an exhibitionist in that regard. It was reminiscent of those who served under George Washington—those who had no shoes and wrapped their feet in rags while fighting the battle of Trenton in winter, but primarily, it was a memorial for those I had served with in the Marines. I hadn't worn shoes since 1972, and this didn't seem an appropriate time to start.

I thought of what those early militiamen had endured fighting for their freedom; they were all in. I couldn't fully know their struggle, having been born with freedom without fighting for it on my own turf, but I had an inkling of an understanding.

My barefoot walk across America was the only way I knew to express my own brand of patriotism.

VETERAN SUICIDE

Our route was a single thread of asphalt pavement in the flag of roads that covered America. Averaging 10 miles a day, I encountered at least one person that lost someone to suicide.

If suicide was a virus taking 18 lives a day, it would be the only thing you would see or hear on the news; you would think the world was ending and we would throw money at it until it was fixed because we'd be afraid we were next. Unfortunately, everyone thinks suicide is something that won't impact them personally. The ultimate truth, however, is that preventing suicide requires effort on everyone's part. It's not a virus, it can't be fixed by a silver bullet, and you can't make money fixing it. Maybe that last bit explains the lack of priority,

Suicide is the tip of an insidious iceberg. Active military members and Veterans combined make up approximately 8% of the US population, but their rate of suicide is elevated in comparison.[4] Private and governmental studies (including those collected by the VA) indicate rates of homelessnes[5], PTSD[6], depression[7],Intimate Partner Violence (IPV) for both male and female Veterans[8], and substance use disorders[9] for the military, and Veteran populations are all elevated in comparison to the general population.

It affects not only active military personnel and Veterans but all of us. We are all on the perimeter of the impact zone.

Mark Twain once said, "There are lies, damn lies, and statistics." The statistics are just numbers until you put a face to them. Then it becomes a person whose story you have witnessed or (as on my walk) heard.

Perhaps we should all look a bit closer or listen a bit more intently.

---

[4] https://www.nami.org/Advocacy/Policy-Priorities/Improve-Care/Protecting-Veterans-Access-to-Mental-Health-Care
https://www.research.va.gov/topics/homelessness.cfm
[5] http://nchv.org/index.php/news/media/background_and_statistics/
https://www.hsrd.research.va.gov/news/feature/homelessness-2020.cfm
[6] https://www.nami.org/Advocacy/Policy-Priorities/Improve-Care/Protecting-Veterans-Access-to-Mental-Health-Care
https://www.nami.org/Your-Journey/Veterans-Active-Duty
[7] https://www.nami.org/Your-Journey/Veterans-Active-Duty
[8] https://www.hsrd.research.va.gov/publications/esp/partner_violence-report.pdf
https://www.womanshealth.va.gov/womenshealth
[9] https://www.mentalhealth.va.gov/docs/2016suicidedatareport.pdf

WHO CARES

During the first week of my walk, I stopped at a Federal building in Wellesley, MA to gather signatures. I was told, "We don't have a problem," and was asked to leave.

So, I continued my route through a low-income housing area, where an inch-and-a-half piece of broken headlight glass tried to escape the neighborhood by hiding in my foot.

After surgically removing it with my fingers, packing it with dirt (which has more uses than people give it credit for) to stop the bleeding, and taking a moment to recoup after getting a cold sweat and wave of nausea, I was good to go.

I thought to myself, *I quit my job and sold my stuff for pennies on the dollar to walk over 3,000 miles. I can't do this. I must be out of my mind. What was I thinking? Who cares? What can I do? I can't do anything. I got thrown out of a Federal Building, my foot hurts, my escort is going off the deep end and I'm starting to believe I am too.*

Wah, wah, wah, my mind kept the broken record going.

⸻◆•◆•◆⸻

I must be out of my mind.

A PLOT OF GRASS

In the middle of my pity parade, I called my brother to whine about questioning my sanity. "Don't worry," he said, "We question it too, and nobody asked you to do this."

When the conversation ended, I thought, "No one asked me. It's my choice." I zoned out and kept walking until I found myself looking at a green, well-kept lawn. It was one and a half feet by four feet, weeded, watered by hand, and cut with a lawnmower—in the middle of a slum.

Stopping, I wondered what the landowner was thinking. Everyone else's yard was the same size—no larger than a postage stamp—made up of pounded dirt with trash, broken-down cars, and telephone poles as fixtures. The houses were so close together that you couldn't fit a NY phone book between them.

I laughed at first, thinking whoever cared for that lawn must be crazy and stupid because they had bought a lawn-mower to cut six square feet of grass and spent all that time and effort in a crappy neighborhood. *Why? What statement are they making? Do they really care? Does it matter?*

Whatever the reason, I began to tell myself, If they can do that and not worry about what others think, then why can't I walk across America?

I decided, *I will walk today and see how I feel tomorrow.* Walking one day at a time took away the immensity of my journey.

It slowly started to crystalize that I was crucifying myself by trying to please others without knowing what they wanted—and not giving any thought to what I wanted. That plot of grass was the catalyst that inspired me to unchain myself from my negative thoughts and find what made me happy and motivated to continue with the walk.

THE ZOMBIE

One night, Paulie told me he would walk with me and asked, "How is it—doing it barefoot?"

"It's no big deal because of the grass, sand, grade, and pavement—nothing like walking the AT." He decided if I could do it, then he could too.

We set off barefoot, talking along the way about his teenage daughter, who told him, "Everyone says I'm a jerk, but my friend, she really gets me." He told me that he responded, "Yeah, 20 people think you're an asshole, but this one girl gets you. Guess what: she's an asshole too!" That was another example of the human tendency (well known to me) to find excuses for negative behavior—not caring what others thought and not knowing what it did to those around me, as well as to myself.

We stopped along our route to get a drink at a Mom and Pop deli. The pretty girl behind the counter smiled at Paulie, who took it as a sign that she was really into him. He didn't need a wingman, so I stepped outside to sip my drink and keep an eye on my sign.

A young man needing a shave barreled up in a loud black muscle car needing a paint job. He got out of the vehicle, wearing all black and walking with an attitude, and stomped into the deli. Another entitled kid—I'm guessing he didn't get chocolate milk in his cereal this particular morning. Shortly after, he stormed out with his purchase and slid back into his car. He looked up from the steering wheel and stared at the sign next to me. A moment later, he got out of his car, walked toward me like a zombie, and said, "I did it. It's my fault."

"What are you talking about?"

"My brother came home and committed suicide. He told us he was gonna, but I didn't believe him. It's my fault. He left two sons behind. They're all messed up. It destroyed our whole family."

Looking into his eyes, I saw the windows of an empty house that would never be the same. If you're only as healthy as the sickest person in the room, what chance does this family have? I regretted my hasty judgment, having pegged him as some spoiled teenager—another example of not knowing.

He got back into his car and drove away while I stood there at a loss, wondering what I could have done for him.

Paulie exited the deli (mating ritual complete), and we continued hiking until he began to lag behind. I turned around just in time to see him stumble and asked, "What's the matter?"

"I can't walk. My feet are killing me." I offered to walk back and get the car for him, but he refused. "I'll hitchhike back."

It's difficult for me to be around ill or injured people because, as a child, I was punished for being sick and was told I was making it up to get out of work. The day I puked while doing yard work, my father finally believed me. So, when people around me are sick or hurt, I usually disappear until they recover. It's not that I don't care, but more like I don't know what to do—don't know how to fix it.

I left him standing on the other side of the road. Two hours later, he pulled up in his car, got out wearing a pair of shoes, and finished the day with me.

"You know, I felt a little bad about your feet," I said.

"Yeah? What would make you feel really bad? Two bloody stumps?"

"Yeah, that would do it," I confirmed.

"Nice."

For the next week, he would have trouble walking until his feet healed.

Looking into his eyes, I saw the windows of
an empty house that would never be the same.

A MOTHER'S LITANY

The following day was beautiful in Massachusetts: not too bright, and it was cool with low humidity. A man in his forties stopped his car on an overpass, got out, and read me the riot act. "Check out your facts! Only two die a week. I'm in the Army Reserves. I know." There was no talking to him, though I tried. He refused to sign the petition and sped off. I wondered if I was on a fool's errand or if I was simply a fool.

About 10 minutes later, a car passed me and made a hasty u-turn. A woman got out and stood there like a steel rail shot into the ground, unmovable, as she looked at me through tear-filled eyes. When I got to her, her eyes lowered and she pleaded for me to help her son, who had come home from deployment a complete stranger and had been redeployed, even after being diagnosed with PTSD. "Every day, I wait for the phone to ring and tell me he's dead." She hugged me.

It didn't matter if two Veterans die every week or eighteen a day; one might be her son. I didn't know at the time, but this would be a typical encounter for me—to be held by a thousand mothers as if I was the child they lost or feared losing, while they blamed themselves for what happened.

When a child dies by their own hands, the parents ask themselves: Where did I fail? Why did they do this? Where did I go wrong? What could I have done? Why didn't I see this? Didn't I know this child?

The event creates a sense of personal accountability and the litany becomes: It's my fault. He told me. I didn't believe him. I should've known. It's my fault.

You may think to yourself, after reading this far, that you could have stopped it or done something differently. But when you're in it, it's a completely different world. It isn't the same person you knew before their experience—a person who would have never have even contemplated suicide, much less completed it.

If that's you, please hear me: it's not your fault. You never went through what they did or saw the world the way they did. You have no clue of the depth of their suffering, so you try to treat them like you always had. Denial and lack of understanding have become the horsemen of your apocalypse, but a time will come (perhaps it is now) when you will be able to lay down the guilt.

AMERICAN LEGION

It was an overcast morning in Connecticut as I plowed through a bumper crop of poison ivy, the cash crop for calamine lotion. At ten in the morning, I found myself in front of an American Legion Hall with a good number of cars parked outside. What a great place to get some signatures.

Walking up to the door, I heard music, glasses clinking, and lively discussions. I opened the door and stood still, allowing my eyes to adjust to the dark as the sound of silence greeted me and men looked at me sideways. By the time I got to the bar, the music shut off, breathing stopped, and the place became a wax museum. I looked at each of the pantomimes and explained that I was gathering signatures for a petition to get mandatory counseling and other services for military members and Veterans.

I experienced deja vu. I saw myself delivering a sermon at the pulpit (the bar), to the choir (other Vets), polishing the alter by dragging eight ounces of holy water (booze) at a time. I had believed that, in its consumption, I could wipe out the past, only to find it never consumed the past. Rather, it allowed the past to consume me. My sermons were all built on the same foundation: It's not my fault. I didn't do it. They should do something about it.

After speaking at them, I realized I had invaded their sanctuary—a place where no action was necessary. I had done the unspeakable, calling them to action, while peer pressure froze them in place. I placed the petition on their alter, giving them an opportunity to look it over, and left without hearing a murmur.

The politically correct amount of distance and time passed before one could talk behind another's back. When my last foot went over the door saddle, the music started, and it was like I had never been there.

LOST

The next day, I woke up and went to my command post (the table in our 24-foot Warrior Series Winnebago that transformed into a bed). While refueling with leftovers, I mapped out my route and determined where Valeria would pick me up at the end of the day, after she dropped me off where I had concluded yesterday's walk.

I made sure I had the petition, a pen, some water, and a few dollars to get something to eat. Then I was ready to go. The day's route would take me to the center of Middletown, CT, where we would head west to continue across the country. I found comfort in confirming that we were on the right path by neurotically observing road signs and checking the map so often I wore holes in the creases. I didn't want to do extra miles simply because I got lost. I had a timeline to avoid walking through the desert in the summer.

Nevertheless, a few hours into the day's walk, I realized I was off course. I found myself standing in front of a postage-stamp-sized park. It was squished between two old concrete structures and had a cement retaining wall to keep it from spilling onto the sidewalk. I took out my map to determine the correct direction.

A woman was sitting on the wall, unaware it was alive, sipping coffee from a paper cup, and smoking a cigarette. I told her what I was doing and she signed the petition.

I was about to refer to my map again when I noticed a bunch of homeless men drinking and raising hell. I was going to leave without speaking to them (Why bother? What do they care?), but one of them waved me forward with a sense of enthusiasm I couldn't ignore.

One man asked, "What are you doing?"

After I explained, they all signed the petition and started telling me about their military service. One said he had been in the Army.

"That's okay," I said, "I still love you."

There was a heartbeat of stunned silence, and then he yelled, "A fucking jar head!" Thus the banter and camaraderie began. One's brother had been in the USMC and came home with no legs, only to die of an overdose within a year.

The one that waved me over, a Marine, said, "You've inspired me to do something. If you can walk barefoot across America, I can do something."

ANGRY YOUNG VETS

When I turned to leave, they all stood up, shook my hand, and wished me luck. The one whose brother had died donated an amount that, for most, wouldn't cover the cost of lunch, but it was all the money he had.

As I left the park at ten in the morning, I realized that, at the same time the previous day, I was ignored at the American Legion, where I thought I would find support. A day later, I had found myself in an unexpected area, supported by those I would've discarded. You'd think I would have learned my lesson by now but it seems there was no end to the depth of my willful ignorance.

After consulting my map, it was apparent that I hadn't taken the turn I wanted. I retraced my steps until I found the correct intersection. I didn't understand how I could have missed it; the associated road sign had grazed the top of my head when I had walked under it the hour before.

My eyes welled up as it dawned on me: I'm never lost; I just don't always know where I am. I had judged and discounted those men when they were the reason for my mission. If I were to be their voice, I would have to look past my preconceived notions. I had viewed the homeless as people that had given up when it was me who had given up on them.

Many young Veterans driving past me expressed their anger with a curse and a one-finger salute. I had interfered in their lives by bringing something to light: memories wrought with anger, guilt, and shame.

By joining the military, I had placed myself in a situation that went against what I was taught: we are to love our fellow man, and killing another human for any reason is a sin (the way I was taught and believed). I found myself in that moment with no good options. I was unwilling to kill and, therefore, unable to protect my band of brothers from harm's way. I felt like a hypocrite, doing what I was told to do stateside, merely waiting for discharge.

I judged myself guilty and proceed to pass sentence. I had considered shortening my life sentence with a quick suicide, as opposed to the slow one of a life with no joy. The guilt and confusion I carried from my youth, compounded by the feeling of continual betrayal by authoritative figures (the lies, deceptions, secrets, misinformation, hypocrisy, and lack of transparency that hid agendas and placed me in situations with no right answer), developed into mistrust. Are even noble acts shrouded in lies?

After the acts of war were over, it seemed to me, because I remembered more of the negative encounters than the positive, that society sang another tune: you are unlovable monsters. I feel we were discarded, like a set of worn tires, and treated with looks of contempt. Harsh whispers excluded us from the life we left behind—the life we could never find again.

Denied reentry into the life we left, we had to beg for our promised benefits, some of which never materialized. Society's new song swirled around in my head and touched every facet of my life.

I embedded John Q. Public's reaction (to me and other Vietnam-era servicemen) into my psyche, deepening the moral injury. I shouldered the blame, and my life became a car I drove. I endlessly looked in the rearview mirror for a destination, my foot on the brake pedal of guilt, stopping me dead in the road with a full tank of rage. Others who could compartmentalize or, better yet, knew there was nothing to forgive, were able to enjoy the road on which they drove, with a clear destination ahead.

Most of the time, my anger drove people away, but it was one of the few emotions I could feel; if I wasn't really angry, I thought I was happy because I wasn't yelling or ready to hit someone. Let's just say a smile wasn't a feature my face knew. When I let anger define me, I struck out at everything and became a monster, reinforcing what others believed me to be. I was incarcerated in a prison of that single emotion, sponsored by guilt, and sought my release.

I made the mistake of carrying my anger so long that it defined me. Am I what I'm doing or am I what I've done? Am I the man that tucked his children into bed at night or am I the man that struck out in fear?

I've come to believe that I am all those things, but I don't have to let one action or period define my life, but to strive to be better than who I was yesterday.

I have taken the opportunity to examine my life under a microscope by writing this book. The process has been instrumental in shifting my perspective and recognizing the moments in my life where I believed what others believed about me. I defined myself through the clouded lens of their misperceptions, causing me to pretend I was something other than what I am: a loving man that made a mistake, doing the best he could at the time.

These ideas are easy to write when no gears are engaged, or buttons pushed. Using these hard-gained insights to guide me, acknowledging my negative and destructive emotions, recognizing their origins, and overcoming my cultural training of judgment, condemnation, and punishment is taking a lifetime.

I continue to release the self-guilt, anger, and judgment by being of service and forgiving the me I see in others. And I know I am not alone in having struggled. This struggle is shared by many soldiers from the Vietnam War era. Is it fair that a small percentage of people in our country (Veterans, active military members, and their families) suffer the consequences of war on behalf of the rest, and are then treated with resentment?

I feel even today's soldiers get the same song and dance, lies and misperceptions, only it's politically corrected—diluted with two parts respect and one part fear because, well, it's war.

I judged myself guilty and proceeded to pass sentence.

VIETNAM

At the end of my walk for the day, I found a young man staring at me from across the street. When we made eye contact, he ran across the street toward me, as if nothing else existed. Upon reaching me, he asked, "Were you in Vietnam?"

"No," I said.

He got quiet and his shoulders sagged as he told me that he had been in Hanoi. His eyes stopped searching mine for the answer he wouldn't find and instead sought response from a spot in space a gaze could not see. I looked at him, noticing that he was Vietnamese, and realized I had seen that look in his eyes before.

It was 2004, and I was diving to recover the bodies of two young men off a small boat that had sunk while running cod lines off Montauk in February. It took us a full day to get to the site because of the rough seas. My partner got hurt when he was thrown into the railing as we jumped into the water, so I dove the 180 feet alone on regular air.

I was narced[10] by the time I made it to the bottom and sighted the sunken vessel. It was covered with fishhooks from tubs of longlines for cod fishing, and one had snagged me. I'd be damned if I die without a will and leave my ex-wife everything. Slowly back-peddling, I dislodged the hook before it set. Keeping a safe distance, I circled the open boat but was unable to find the bodies.

When I returned to the surface and was safely aboard again, the Captain told me that the family wanted to talk to me when we got back to shore. The father and wives (one with a newborn) met me at the dock for any news I could give them. I was unable to provide closure or put their hopes and fears to rest. They had the same look in their eyes as the guy who crossed the road and asked if I had been in Vietnam.

It was those looks of unbearable emptiness that made me think of what had happened when we were in their country and what continues to happen elsewhere.

We always hear the casualty report of the troops, but not of the civilians. According to Wikipedia, of all the people killed in wars, over 67% are civilians. Looking up statistics for the Vietnam War, I found the

---

[10] Exhibiting impaired judgment while scuba diving due to nitrogen narcosis.

estimates vary widely depending on if casualties in Cambodia and Laos were included and whose statistics you looked at.

The unarmed civilians in a war are the only group in the race without a pony.

———◆•◆•◆———

... of all the people killed in wars, over 67% are civilians.

THE BROOKLYN BRIDGE

Walking over the Brooklyn Bridge for the first time was unlike anything I expected. The day of my crossing was sunny with cotton candy clouds framed in a bright blue sky. I had gone over the bridge in a car before but never realized there was a walkway of old wooden planks on top. The bridge afforded a phenomenal view of the city, which looked like a miniature compared to its overwhelming size when I walked through its streets in canyons of concrete.

I was only on the bridge for a few minutes when I met my first skinhead. At first, I thought he was a fighter: his shirt was off, his head was shaven, and he sported many tattoos, the most notable ink across his stomach. I squinted at his stomach to see what it said, but (being almost legally blind in most states) I had to close the distance.

When I was finally close enough, I saw that it said, "Fuck the world." I guessed he probably was not a fighter because, when I looked at his face, he wasn't moving fluidly, like a wary animal assessing all those in his parameter. I did, however, sense the heat of disjointed hate and rage as he stomped up to me, yelling unintelligibly. My response was to greet him in Polish.

He looked at me confused.

"I thought you were Russian since I didn't understand you."

He stormed away and, an instant later, ran back up to my face, stopped inches away, peering into my eyes, and yelled, "Repent!"

"I am."

He screamed, "Pray to [a name I didn't understand and couldn't have spelled if I tried, though I'm sure it had a few Z's and Q's]," and then left. His rage washed over me like a hurricane's waves on a shore. I hadn't felt rage like that in a long time.

Not far from that encounter, I came upon an African American woman dressed in what appeared to be the fashion of her culture. She looked at my sign and then looked at me with hate-filled eyes. "They will open their eyes in hell," she said with venom. At that point, I felt we don't have to die to go to hell; some have already created our own on Earth.

A Korean Vet saw my sign and, with the bitterness of medicine, said, "They should tough it out. I did. Anyway, they get paid a lot more than I did—so, that's just too bad." He turned his back on me when I started to speak, which surprised me because I thought he would understand. There certainly is a strange and angry group of people crossing that bridge.

On the other side of the bridge, I stopped in a deli for a drink and talked to the two Muslim owners about religion and politics. We agreed on almost everything.

"It's too bad we spend so much time focusing on our differences," they said, "and not on our similarities." They donated and I hadn't even asked—another surprise, as I thought they wouldn't (while others I thought would, didn't).

His rage washed over me
like a hurricane's waves on a shore.

A CRY FOR HELP

I got an email stating that walking barefoot was a cry for help. Yes, it is a cry for help. On this walk, the tales of grief, sobbed by those left behind, echoed what my father said. "If you don't cry, you don't care."

Every day of my journey across America, I published blogs about America's tears. Veterans and family members shared meals or mere moments on the side of the road with me, crying as they mourned their loved ones lost to war. On this walk, hearing so many expressions of grief, my walls began to crumble. I cried every day for ten and a half months. I held mothers whose grief became my own as we asked ourselves, "What could I have done to prevent that enormous loss?"

Anyone who asks himself, "If the voice I listen to in my head were a person, would it be my friend?" and answers no, is also crying out for help.

Yes, my actions were a call for help from the edge of despair. You couldn't assist me if you didn't hear my cry. I hoped people would respond by helping one person or writing one letter to the government. I hoped people would join me in changing the world for the many that suffered—especially for Veterans.

When we were little and had to dry the dishes after my mom washed them, my father would play his harmonica and sing a WWII song called, "The Postman Delivered a Letter." He sang it to make us cry. The song was about the last letter a soldier wrote to his mother. I used to think he did it so we would have to take more time wiping our tears off the dishes as he watched and laughed.

I figure my grandfather never cried for my father, so my father never felt loved by him. I now believe my father got out of us what he was unable to get out of his father—he could make us cry—it had an impact on us he could see, hear, and touch (our tears). It didn't matter, though; he didn't believe us.

MISSING WALLET

Arriving back at the camper after roasting my soles over asphalt and cement, I found Valeria crying at the table. I asked her what was wrong, and she said, "I just got an email from a man you met walking today." She began to read it to me:

I was discharged from the military recently, 6 by 2 [active duty and reserves]. I haven't cried in eight years. Even after my father's passing six years ago, I just held it in... I cried today, after I met Ron. Thank you and Godspeed.

She cried uncontrollably. Uncomfortable with her display of emotion, I asked, "You know why he cried after I left?"

"No," she sniffled.

"Because after I left, his wallet was missing."

"You asshole."

At least she stopped crying.

Writing this book has continued to give me insight and clarity as to who I was, who I am, and who I want to be. Being brought up 'tough' made me ignore my feelings, substituting them with a distraction.

Making jokes out of tragedy was (and still is) an effective method to prevent myself from displaying emotion and it helps distract me from feeling.

I'm still a work in progress.

This realization that I had a habit that no longer served me at this time in my life was the inspiration for Challenge 7 replacing old habits with new ones. What habits do you have that don't serve you well anymore? In the back of the book all the challenges are listed for you to take your own inward journey.

CHARACTER

I was first asked, "what is the essence of your character," by a Berkeley college professor, whose brother I had met at a Veterans' retreat. I had mentioned that I was writing a book about my walks along the Appalachian Trail and across the country. I thought my character was me: a loner, tough as a two-bit steak.

After a couple of weeks of contemplation, I realized who I actually was: a man with an enormous burden of guilt, gifted by his father (a man who always needed someone to blame). I was also a man becoming aware that he was breaking the cycle of guilt, shame, and anger by transferring the force behind that cycle to passion, service, and honor. The result of my self-healing would (hopefully) be an inspiration to others to forgive themselves for a life squandered.

Without realizing it, I had allowed myself to feel when I cried while holding a grieving mother. I was able to be present in that moment without making a joke to deflect my feelings.

Five years after the walk across America, I called Valeria. I had watched her experience extreme emotional lability during our time together, but she always had my back. I asked her to forgive me for not appreciating what she went through to complete that trip with me.

Until then, I had not understood her perspective—why she acted the way she did or the sacrifice she made—until a man explained it to me. "Ron, every time you were drunk, you were temporarily bipolar."

I got it. That was the first time I could relate to it.

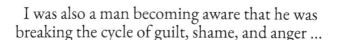

I was also a man becoming aware that he was
breaking the cycle of guilt, shame, and anger ...

ARE YOU RIGHT WITH THE LORD?

As I journeyed through the Bible Belt, I was often asked, "Who do you work for: God or Satan?" With just one look at me, it seemed people had already made up their minds. One morning, a woman was standing in front of her house with arms crossed and head held high, and she looked down on me with a self-righteous smirk and asked, "Are you right with the Lord?"

I looked her dead in the eyes and said the first thing that came to mind. "I'm glad you asked because he sent me to see you today."

Her smirk evaporated like mist in the sun as she lowered her head and dropped her arms to her side. Defeated, she asked, "What do you want?"

"A few dollars and a little to eat would be nice."

"Wait here." She turned around and went into the house. A moment later, a lanky teenage boy, wearing a t-shirt, jeans, and a smile, emerged from the house and handed me two dollars and a small cup of yogurt. I thanked him and, as I ate his offering, told him what the walk was about. Then I left without kicking the dust off my feet.

After that, I was still asked if I was right with the Lord, but I freed myself from confrontation by not defending or attacking. What a novel thought.

A billboard on my route read, "He who has the Lord needs nothing else." I wondered whether the author was saying that before or after he already had everything else.

That's an easy statement to make when you have it all, but what about Veterans coming back to no job and no family? Are they the saints, living under bridges? I remember thinking the God that billboard mentioned is the one that greets them at death when there's no need of the things they pray for daily.

I don't consider myself an expert on religious matters. At times, my faith in God has been weak, but it was still there. On the other hand, there have also been many moments during which I've completely lost my faith in my fellow man. People often tell me they believe in God, but I think they only mean they believe there is one. All religions write about truth; you just have to read between the lines to find it.

DIVORCE

At the post office in Daggett, California, I got a local to sign my petition. While we were standing there, a man with two children said he also wanted to sign it. His father had been a Marine in the Korean War and, as a child, he remembered being awakened in the middle of the night by his dad screaming in his sleep. His father drank, which did nothing to stop the nightmares, but it made his childhood memorable.

Before passing through Daggett, two young men in military uniforms asked if I was Ron. When I confirmed, they shook my hand and said, "Thank you. We saw you walking, looked up your website and we have been calling you 'Barefoot Ron' ever since."

I told them the plan. "We need tools to make it home and reconnect with our families. A high percentage of Veteran suicides are because of a failed relationship. When we return home, everyone knows we're different except us."

One smiled and said, "I got divorced after my first deployment. The first one is the toughest, but after you've lived through it and do it again, it's your new normal. I never thought about what you proposed, but it makes a lot of sense."

He continued, "One of my friends committed suicide after his first deployment. We see that most of the suicides are from guys after their first trip over. After your second or third, you get used to the boredom and the crazy stuff and the chicken shit, and the nightmares start to go away."

Prior to my encounter with the two active Soldiers in Daggett, Valeria and I had a visit from a wife and son of a Soldier who happened to see our camper parked outside of an RV sales store. She thanked us and said, "I don't want to seem unpatriotic, but I was glad when he went back overseas. I had trouble dealing with him for any length of time because he had changed so much. A lot of wives feel this way, but won't speak up because of how it would sound."

MARRIAGE NUMBER ONE

After returning home from the USMC, living in the woods, and going to college, I met a girl and she came back to Long Island with me after graduation. She told me she couldn't live without me; I hoped she could. She wanted to get married; I didn't. Unskilled at clear verbal communication, I used what I knew (passive aggression) to get my way: I cheated on her. I didn't have the courage to tell her that I didn't want to get married. I figured when I told her what I had done, she would simply leave.

Instead, she said she would kill herself if I didn't marry her. I wasn't prepared for someone so codependent, but who else would have me? At the time, I felt guilty and that my only way out was to marry her. I rationalized that it couldn't be so bad; she didn't make my eyes bleed (she was actually quite beautiful when she smiled) and sex was a given.

On the day of the wedding, Tony (my best man and childhood friend) spent the day with me as I asked for signs to call off the wedding. First, we jumped off a bridge into the canal. I thought if I got hurt I wouldn't be able to go through with it. Next, we drove for a mile on the railroad track. I figured, if the train came, that was a sign. If alcohol or drugs weren't involved in any of these decisions, they should have been. Finally, on the church steps, I stood outside and asked God to stop it. Not getting an answer on the spot, I went ahead with the wedding.

When the priest said, "until death do you part," I vowed to myself that I would do the best I could. My decision also anchored me to my hometown and helped me keep my mom afloat by being the sole operator of the family business.

After a year of marriage, while I was still drinking heavily, we decided to have a child. One day, when my wife was seven months pregnant, we went out, and I had a few drinks. Words were exchanged on the drive home. I parked the car in the driveway, she got out and walked ahead of me to the house, and more words were exchanged.

All of a sudden, she turned around and slapped me in the face. I saw red. The next thing I knew, I was kneeling over her with one hand on her throat and a fist overhead. The red fog instantly dispersed, and I realized what was happening. I laughed to myself in that moment of recognition—I had become my father. I got up and walked away. My wife was furious, as I hadn't done what she expected, which was to hit her, allowing her to confirm I was a monster. That was the moment I quit drinking, swearing again I wouldn't be my old man to my children.

I think the breaking point was a loan for half a million dollars to expand the scuba shop with a gym ... and to throw a bachelor party. She wasn't in favor of the loan; the amount scared her. After taking out the loan, I asked her to give me a year to build it and start recouping our expense. It took longer. I agreed to put all our assets, most of which I had acquired before I met her, in both our names (per her request) as protection for her and the children.

After one year and one month post-loan, the gym addition wasn't yet complete, and one of my employees was getting married. I wanted to throw him a bachelor party. I told my wife we were going to hire a female stripper. "Then you're not going," she said matter-of-factly.

I went anyway.

That night, when I returned home, we sat in the kitchen and she asked me if I was emotionally aroused by the stripper. I answered, "Yes, but I never touched her." She asked me if I believed in the Bible, and I answered yes.

"In the Bible, it says, 'if you look upon a woman with lust, you have committed adultery.'"

"It also says in the Bible to forgive."

"I don't believe in the Bible."

The day after that confrontation occurred, I asked her why she married me.

"For money and convenience." She might as well have stuck an ice pick in my chest.

"Then let's get divorced."

Less than a month later, I was served divorce papers. Her unhappiness with the marriage and her process of getting a divorce was a complete surprise to me. The last year of our marriage had been awesome.

Had her behavior changed because she had decided to get a divorce and devised a plan to take me for all she could, first by luring me into a false sense of security? We had also been experiencing an unprecedented degree of intimacy at that time; my lower brain had never been so happy.

The night after our kitchen conversation, my wedding band exploded and split in half on my finger. I knew in that moment I didn't have to wait until "Death do us part;" the marriage was over.

She got everything in the divorce: four houses, full medical, alimony, child support, the car, gas for the car, and continuing education payments. It all paled in comparison, though, to the fact that she got custody of my two sons.

Part of me wanted to believe that she had planned it to appear as a divorce when she was really just securing our assets so we wouldn't lose everything if I failed with the gym. If that was her initial plan, though, she never told me. After the divorce, my desire to believe that folly allowed me to continually punish myself, thinking I had a chance and blew it. Hindsight isn't always 20/20.

Hindsight isn't always 20/20.

DIVORCE NUMBER ONE

At the beginning of the divorce, while still in shock, I thought it would be best to disappear from my children's lives, convinced my ex would find another man—a better man—to raise them. I decided to tell my oldest that I loved him and to say goodbye, so I went to the schoolyard where he was playing and called him over.

"Your mother and I are getting a divorce. I'm leaving and I won't see you again." He just stood there and cried. Instantly, I felt horrible and knew no one could love him as I did; I would always be his father.

Until putting this story to paper, I had never realized I was what I swore I'd never be: my father. I had done to my son what my father had done to me—I made him cry. From that moment on, I swore to be there for my sons.

At that time in my life, I made no attempt to hide my anger, unleashing it on everybody. I contemplated killing my wife and foolishly started verbalizing my intent to other people. In doing so, I scared myself because, for me, it's a short walk from saying it to making it a reality.

With my twisted Catholic mentality, still trying to avoid hell, I turned it around and made a pact with God.

"Hey, God, I'm going to give you a gift."

What can you give a guy who has everything?

"I'm not going to think about my ex for two weeks."

After the first week, I cried, realizing the gift was to myself. Killing her would end with me dead or in prison, and my boys would be messed up orphans that might even take their own lives.

LIFE SPRING

During the first year of my divorce, my sister checked in on me regularly. She had gone to an empowerment retreat at Life Spring six months prior and raved about what it had done for her. "You've got to go!"

I told her I would, but didn't plan on acting on it. This went on for a couple of weeks until she called and, fed up with the pestering, I said, "I'm going," to put her off.

She told me I wouldn't have to worry about it—that she had already paid for it. At the time, I didn't have money problems (yet), but my sister, who ran out of gas in Myrtle Beach while fleeing from her ex who had threatened her life, was having both monetary and health issues. I didn't learn until later on that, to raise the money for my attendance, she raffled off everything of value she had left after fleeing her husband.

At the graduation ceremony following the Life Spring retreat, the graduates stood with their eyes closed, lights low, and soft music playing. Then we were told to open our eyes to see someone who cares about us and is here for us. I didn't expect anyone to be there for me, having burnt those bridges.

Nevertheless, I opened my eyes and saw my sister standing before me; I was stunned. Ever since then, I have trouble envisioning my sister walking through doorways, on account of her angel wings. She had ridden 16 hours one way on a Greyhound to see me for one hour; she paid for the trip by picking up soda cans on the side of the road.

The retreat and recognizing someone cared was a major turning point, getting me out of victimhood. It's easy to give lip service and say, "I love you," but to take action that screams so loud the deaf can hear is a whole other thing. A few days after getting home from the seminar, I called my ex-wife and said, "I hope someday you can forgive me for blaming you when things went wrong, being mean to you, and taking you for granted." It was the only time she didn't attack me. She simply hung up.

I realized that saying I was sorry didn't mean anything if I didn't know what I was sorry for. That moment, owning 100% of the divorce (because if I had been different she never would have acted the way she did towards me) I was free.

Owning my actions took away my ability to blame others for all the trouble in the world. It was both freeing to know no one makes me do anything and burdening to be aware of my power.

After my call to my ex-wife, I made another to my ex-girlfriend, Robin. We made arrangements to meet at dusk on the beach near her house. I had always thought of Robin as a genius. She could gain insight into someone's personality after talking to them for just five minutes—a gift she wasted. At the beach, I quietly apologized for all the things I had done and failed to do. I also told her about the empowerment retreat I had attended and encouraged her to go, thinking it would resonate with her. After we parted, she called my family to ask if I was dying because, during her encounter with me, I was out of character.

She did go to the empowerment retreat and she even went beyond that, becoming an inspirational trainer and life coach. She started her own international company: Momentum. Seven years later, she died. Over 2000 people she had empowered with her service attended her funeral.

I went to the service and, while sitting in the pew, thought about the few people who would have attended our funerals if we had died when we first met. Those attending hers would have said, "What a waste. She had so much talent," and the few at mine would have come just to make sure I was dead.

Both Robin and I ultimately came to believe that acceptance, healing, love, and action are the sparks that set the world on fire.

Everything matters: every word, action, and thought. We don't simply help people; we empower them to live by being the example with our lives.

I just had a long way to go.

This was a major turning point in my life, taking accountability for my actions and doing my best to amend or at least acknowledge them to those I had hurt. What actions are you owning up to and how will you do that? In the back of the book all the challenges are listed for you to take your own inward journey. This event was the basis for Challenge 6: Apologizing.

MARRIAGE NUMBER TWO

God has always been very persistent in giving me an opportunity to learn a lesson. Sometimes, I wished He wasn't so good to me, but how else was I going to get it?

My second marriage ended in divorce, ten years after the relationship started and only two years into the marriage. Obviously, I hadn't learned how to make a marriage work. How could I make someone else happy when part of me felt unworthy? I wasn't even conscious that I projected this belief onto the relationship, making me unable to love another. What a convoluted way of keeping myself isolated and miserable.

Even now, I'm disheartened that I have no friendly relationship with my second wife, as well as my first. I can only tell myself that we loved one another the best we could at the time.

———◆•◆•◆———

How could I make someone else happy when
part of me felt unworthy?

WALKING ON COALS: SHANKSVILLE, PA

I was unceremoniously dropped off on the side of the road in northern Pennsylvania during a month-long heat wave of 100+ degrees. The walk took a toll on civility and humor in our home-on-wheels. In the direct sun, the blacktop reached temperatures over 150 degrees, hot enough to cook an egg in less than five minutes. By noon, the smell of bacon with no deli in sight was a warning my feet were cooking!

On the first day of walking in that temperature, the heat went up to my knees like a misguided sledgehammer hitting my feet, triggering the stages of shock, nausea, sweating, and tunnel vision. That prompted me to, on subsequent days, start before the sun was up in order to mark off miles and avoid most of the extreme heat.

I did my best to walk on sand, grass, or the white line, which was at least a few degrees cooler than the blacktop. Sometimes, I was amazed at how grateful I was for those little things.

The challenge of walking in that burning heat took me back to a memorable bonding moment with my father when I was eight. Early one Saturday morning, we were sitting in the kitchen at our yellow Formica and metal table. My father had a shot or two of "gut-rot whiskey" out of a glass (to make it civilized), as he played with his Zippo lighter, getting the flame guard cherry red.

When it had reached his desired color, he said, "Give me your arm." When I did, he held the guard to my forearm, pushing it firmly into my flesh till it sizzled. As he looked into my eyes, I looked at him in wonder and fear, holding back tears (for fear of being punished for crying).

"Why did you do that?"

"To see if you're tough."

I thought I had failed.

I felt a a tear well up in the corner of my eye; I hoped it wouldn't run down my face and disappoint him. Was I weak? Did I have to be tough to be loved?

Looking back, I'm glad he wasn't a cowboy, or he would've branded my ass with a triple Z. I wonder if that was his way of preparing me for the world as he saw it—his way of showing he cared.

KICKED TO THE CURB

While I was out frying my soles on the Pennsylvanian asphalt, Valeria got permission from a Veteran who managed a McDonald's to park in their lot. It was right along our route, so she didn't have to do any extra driving for that day's pick up or the drop off the next morning.

Once I was in the camper, she went on and on about the temperature and how she suffered in the heat as if I had spent the day in an air-conditioned office. Not seeing the dog when sitting down, I accidentally knocked him off the seat and she began screaming at me, telling me to leave in the morning because she couldn't be with a monster that made her dog cry. I slept on the dining area seats that converted into a bed and, in the morning, packed my computer, cell phone, and a change of clothes. On my way out, I noticed a small envelope with my name on it. Isn't that nice—she's considerate enough to send me off with the money that our friend gave us before we left the Keys. After walking a few hours, wondering how I was going to walk the 134 miles to Shanksville in two days for a scheduled speaking engagement, my phone rang.

It was Valeria. "I will stay on this trip because I gave you my word I would. I believe in this cause, even if I no longer believe in you."

I was thrilled about not having to do a major forced march, but sad I was in a relationship that continued to worsen as the miles piled up. I thought she felt like she was competing with the mission for my affection. On top of that, she was constantly bathed in the inherent challenges of the journey, which only acerbated her own weaknesses, which I didn't want to deal with. Unable to live up to her expectations, which seemed to change from instant to instant, and give her the attention she demanded, I stopped trying. When she arrived to pick me up at the end of the day, I thanked her for the ride and the envelope with the money.

"What money?"

I reminded her about the envelope.

"It's from the manager of McDonald's."

Opening it, I saw four McDonald's coupons and laughed. Who has it better than me—kicked to the curb with four happy meals?

I find that, besides deflecting my feelings and emotions, humor can also stop me from taking myself too seriously and shift my perception. It reminds me of a joke I read in Laughter in Hell.

Two soldiers in a concentration camp made a promise to one another that they would find humor each day to help them survive. After a year, they memorized Hitler's route and planned to kill him at noon. Noon came and went and they waited for another half hour.

Then one of them said, "I wonder what happened."

The other responded. "Yeah, I hope he's alright."

Who has it better than me—
kicked to the curb with four happy meals?

7 - DAY ADVENTIST

In West Virginia, I was finally in the mountains, happy to be free of plodding through cities of restless motion that pounded out songs of anxiety. While passing through the mountains, looking out over a sea of green, I felt like I was at the edge of the ocean, observing the vastness and silence that instilled a sense of peace.

The peace was shattered by two men in a bright red pickup truck, pulling up from behind, cutting in front of me to stop my progress. Uniformed in garments fresh off Kmart racks, they jumped out of the truck with a sense of urgency. They began to preach. "The true Lord will come and wipe out all those that believe in the false lord: Money!" They began naming an assortment of well-known people they felt were worshiping that false lord. It sounded like all the people on their list were politicians.

The one yelling the loudest seemed familiar. I realized he had the same fire in his eyes and rage in his heart as the skinhead I had encountered on the Brooklyn Bridge. Maybe they're long-lost brothers.

"What are you doing to save these brothers that have gone down the wrong path?" I inquired.

"Preaching."

"Why are you screaming? Why are you so angry with them? Aren't you happy you're going to heaven? If you're already saved, and not everybody can be saved, why do you even care if they're going to hell?"

The quiet one appeared to be thinking about it and the screamer paused.

"You're scary with all this hate," I continued, "I'd think you'd feel sorry for them since they're going to hell."

That ended his sermon. With no response, they packed up their mobile evangelical crusade and left.

People have asked me a lot of questions about God over the years: If there is a God, how could He allow greed, wars, hate, sickness, and violence to happen? Is free will total, or is it only for the things you think you can control? If God really is in control, wouldn't He want better for me than I want for myself?

I think the cause of all problems may be rooted in fear: fear of scarcity, pain, loss of security or love, or fear of God himself. If I'm afraid of loss, I attack to protect what I think I'm losing. If I'm fearless, what need is there to attack?

Fearing God doesn't make sense to me if you believe God loves all his children. I can't imagine sending my children to hell and, if they were there, I would storm the gates to get them out. I wouldn't want my children to fear me; I wouldn't want them to think I'd harm them. Is that how my evangelical crusaders saw God?

———◆•◆•◆———

I felt like I was at the edge of the ocean, observing the vastness and silence that instilled a sense of peace.

THE CAT

Halfway across a mile-long bridge, I found a gray and white tiger kitten eating something bloody. I bent down and picked him up. He cried when I held him; he had been eating his own tail. I wondered how it came to be alone on the bridge, thinking maybe somebody had dropped a bag full of them into the river under the cover of darkness. As I contemplated whether to throw him over to join his siblings, I noticed a plaque stating the date the bridge was built; it was my birthday.

I believe everything is a sign (unfortunately, I never seem to figure them all out). I now realize how that cat kept my trip in motion by giving Valeria a bright spot to hang onto.

There was no way I was throwing him away, so I put him in the pouch taped to the back side of my sign with the petition. After calling Valeria and telling her about the kitten, I tried to think of ways to convince her to let him join us and the dog on our trip. As soon as we got to the camper, Valeria opened the door and, before I could say a word, the kitten jumped out of the pouch and ran between the dog's legs to her food. That kitten ate so much before we could grab him that he looked like a softball with appendages.

"Can I keep him?"

"Yes," she said. Turns out she had been trying to figure out what to say to convince me to keep him.

The thing that impressed me the most about that cat happened when someone invited us to stay with them for a few days. On the first day we were there, five dogs surrounded the tiny kitten, waiting for it to run. Without fear, he ambled over to the largest dog, eye to eye, grabbed his nose with both paws, and bit him. The dog yelped and took off, followed by the rest.

I dubbed him "the cat" before we found out it was female. I then started calling her "Princess" because she lay on the dashboard like it was the place of honor for traveling royalty. Any cat that fearlessly takes on five dogs has my respect.

STAY OFF THE ROAD

I was walking alone through a densely wooded, sparsely populated area, able to see at least a mile in both directions. I decided to walk in the middle of the street. Seeing a car coming up in the distance, I stepped over to the side of the road. When it finally got to me, I noticed it was a police car. It stopped and the officer got out to tell me I was disrupting traffic. I looked in both directions; we were alone. Leaving, he said, "Stay on the side of the road."

A few miles later, on that warm pleasant day as still as if the wind forgot to breathe, an old pickup truck came from behind. The passenger shot at me! Man are they serious about staying on the side of the road around here!

I was startled but unafraid. The old me would have been mad as hell, ready to fight and get revenge. I would have been afraid that I wasn't getting the recognition I deserved and that I could die for something I had no control over—once again, a victim.

At that moment, I knew that I would die for my belief in this mission because it was worth it to find support for my brothers. I did not need to respond in kind. I was working to ensure peace for returning Veterans. If I fought for it with violence, I would have already lost it.

That day, I felt I really was a Marine. I was in a different kind of combat, by committing my life to my mission—going back for those with the invisible wounds. I was a Marine without a mission no more.

At that moment, I knew that I would die
for my belief in this mission ...

REFORM SCHOOL

Shortly after entering Tennessee, I cruised past a large building with a brick façade and no signage that, for some reason, stood out from the landscape. Looking at it stirred something in the back of my mind—a shadow of a thought I couldn't put words to.

A woman came running out of the building towards me and asked me if I would speak to those inside; it was a reform school. She seemed in a panic, like a mother desperate for help in saving her children. Not knowing how she knew about me (newspaper, word of mouth, window view, etc.), I welcomed the invitation.

Once inside the building, I was led to a nearby room and came face to face with six boys ranging in ages from 15 to 18. Two were seated on a worn upholstered couch and the others were on faded, green, overstuffed chairs in an unadorned, institutional room with tired wooden floors. The atmosphere of the room triggered a memory of the room in our house where my father used to sit and drink. The green, vintage, overstuffed chairs the boys sat in reminded me of my father's chair, and the wooden floor resembled the one he had installed in our own home.

The boys tried to look tough with smirks (aka, shit-eating grins) and arms crossed over their chest. I saw myself in them at that age: angry and defiant. It reminded me of long ago when my best friend was sent away while I stayed behind. I started by telling them who I was and what I was doing and why I was doing it.

Then I just let the words flow without forethought about what I should say or how it should be said. The brain thinks, but the heart knows.

"I used to feel what you're feeling now. I was angry and defiant. Nobody was going to tell me what to do. I was where you are now. I blamed my parents, my teachers, the church, the government—anyone but me. Nothing was my fault. I know now that I became a victim by not taking responsibility for any of my own choices and actions because a victim has no control. I never owned anything bad I did, but I also could never take credit for anything good I did. I could never get anywhere until I quit looking at myself as a victim and took responsibility for my actions.

"Do you have any questions?" Silently, they looked at one another for unspoken approval to speak. I continued, "You may just think I'm some crazy old guy going barefoot. Maybe I am, but I care, and I do what I think is right. I'm honored that you even took the time to listen to me. Thank you."

On my way out to resume my walk, one of the boys followed me and said, "I know what you're talking about because I go to counseling. Thank you." He handed me his well-worn hat as a gift.

After he walked back into the building, the woman who had invited me in came out and thanked me. "I have a couple that think the world owes them. They needed to hear that."

I understood what she meant. We don't believe some who are close to us, no matter what they say, but a stranger can say the same thing and we listen because they haven't given us a reason not to believe them.

When people ask me why their children don't listen to them, I ask them if they remember when they were kids. It's amazing how many people have forgotten when they were children and watched everything their parents did and said. Their actions and words created a foundation for our own future thoughts and behaviors. Any misalignment rocked our world, teaching us about hypocrisy. It's no wonder they don't listen to everything we say and often become rebellious.

I wished there were magic words to transform those boys I met in that reform school. A man who knew my family once came up to me when I was an adult and said, "I don't know how you survived your childhood." Back then, I felt anger. Continuing my walk after speaking to the boys, I felt an overwhelming sense of impotency brought on by a memory of my ex-brother-in-law abusing my nephew.

He stood him on a stool, putting him on display, while he put his face to his and screamed, reprimanding him for some forgettable offense. I remember my nephew trembling uncontrollably as he endured this public shaming and the wrath of his father. I didn't know how to change it, so I accepted it as what was, as did my mother, father, girlfriend, and sister (the boy's mother), all of whom were in the room.

My nephew is now a wanted criminal.

I know now that I became a victim by not taking responsibility
for any of my own choices and actions.

FAMILY

As the reform school got smaller and smaller the farther I walked away, my memories about growing up became larger and larger. I came into the world on Veterans Day the usual way, kicking and screaming, born for my current task in a normal post-war family headed by an alcoholic Vet. Normal was defined as all I knew—a point of reference far from healthy. In my world, the gap between healthy and normal was as great as the abyss between law and justice (second only to the gap between love and hate).

I was the oldest of seven children born to a mother and father, both of Polish descent. My father was drunk, loud, and violent every day. When he was seventeen, he had a choice of four years in prison for armed robbery or an all-expense paid vacation with the 106th Airborne to see Europe. He chose Europe and was there for the last five months of WWII. He used to boast that they enlisted him to end it. After the war, they threw in a bonus tour of Auschwitz, where he got to see our relatives scraped off the floor of ovens—the site that would become a memorial, a shrine denoting unfathomable carnage.

As the first child in the family, I had the privilege of being the experiment and was beaten every day, either physically or verbally, or both. They must have thought the parenting method was successful because my father continued it with each of my siblings until my brother had an unusual series of health scares. When my brother was about six years old, he ran into the street and hit the bumper of a car with his head. When my father ran to get him, he was laying on the street, foaming at the mouth. He survived. Shortly after the accident, my brother became ill and we thought he had cancer. Those two health scares caused a change in my father's behavior. He toned down his hostility towards us.

That caused me some confusion. Did he think my brother would speak unkindly of him at the pearly gates, remembering the treatment he got? Was my father covering all his Catholic bases?

That meant I had to cover all my Catholic bases too. At the time, my confused interpretation was that (1) God loves us unconditionally, but only if we follow all his commandments in thought, word, and deed (otherwise, He doesn't), and (2) loving those that don't love God makes us better than them.

Confession was the safety net, like being home free in a kid's game. If I confessed before I died and was contrite, I'd always be forgiven. The only catch was making it to confession before dying. If my timing was off, there literally would be "hell to pay." That seemed extreme—doing something in an instant, then paying for it for eternity.

Something else happened when my father toned down the brutality toward us. When my siblings had done something that I had been beaten for in the past and were not subsequently punished, I would pick up the slack and do it for him. It didn't seem fair that they weren't getting disciplined.

While growing up, trying to figure out who I was and my place in the world, I was clueless but had enough knowledge to be dangerous. I sought the advice of peers and listened to their opinions as if they knew everything, preferring their honest point of view to my parents' hypocrisy. I rebelled by behaving consistently in line with peoples' low judgment of me. It was along the lines of "If that's what you think I am, I'll show you," only to feel guilty because, deep down, I knew that wasn't me. My own moral compass was nowhere to be found. I would use other people as an excuse for my failures, then be angry about it. I punished myself for endless "should haves" and "could haves." At times, I still do.

The bottom line was that no one was going to tell me what to do or pick on me. I was rebellious, angry, and violent. It was my outlet for the beatings I got at home. It got to the point that mothers from the neighborhood would call my mom to tell her I was fighting with their sons, resulting in another beating when my father got home. That eventually stopped me from fighting in the neighborhood, but not from being angry or rebellious. Later, I would fight in the ring to unleash my anger.

It was odd, because I didn't feel good about hurting someone, so I fought halfheartedly till they wanted to hurt me. Then I would unload. I figured, if I got beat, I deserved it (win/win). I could punish myself mentally for hurting someone or have someone physically do it for me.

Growing up, I lived in the impact zone of a man with post-traumatic stress (PTS). My family life groomed me to become what I hated: a victim, a hypocrite, my father, and 'that angry Veteran with limited tools.' My father's actions were never consistent with what he expected from me. When I was young, I would be my father's hero if I did exactly what he told me, but I also wanted him to be my hero by showing me the right way to be.

The family I was born into afforded me indelible moments that stained all fabrics of my life. Now, I can look at the past with the luxury of time to consider my choices, as compared to moments that demand an immediate response. Little did I know, my tumultuous upbringing would prepare me for a mission in life: to shed light on and help those who found themselves in places similar to those that my upbringing, military experiences, and doomed relationships placed me.

Normal was defined as all I knew—a point of reference far from healthy.

FACE OFF

It was Friday the 13th. I started walking before sunup to beat the full impact of the heat wave, expecting a quiet walk on another still morning. I began thinking about various questions civilians asked me—about why Soldiers end their lives or never talk about their experiences.

I stopped at a convenience store and asked the cashier to sign our petition. She signed it with purpose, as she told me she was worried about her 20-year-old friend home from the war. At first, she told herself that his drinking was because he was partying, glad to be home, but it continued and increased after the initial homecoming. Later, he confided in her that he drank because his buddies were killed and the liquor numbed the pain. One time, when he was drinking, he told her that, in retaliation for his friends' deaths, he tortured a family he thought had played a part in it. He ripped off the faces of their children in front of them before killing them all, one at a time. (I'm told it's a war crime but isn't war a crime?) She was help-less in easing his guilt and she searched my eyes for an answer.

I responded as best I could, "There are times in battle when all of our humanity is lost. Then there are moments when we are our most humane. He deals with his lapse in humanity the only way he knows, and you can't punish him more than he punishes himself, self-medicating as he slowly tortures the monster he believes he is."

The sadness of the story blocked out the quiet morning sun. I could understand how her friend got to that point and how he would carry it to the grave—logic and emotion, in two different camps, engaged in a death battle.

"There are times in battle when all humanity is lost. Then there are moments when we are our most humane."

CONQUERING MY NEGATIVE THOUGHTS

When I was a victim, suicidal thoughts were a comfort. They allowed me to believe I had control over something: the time, the place, and the method of my death. They gave me a small taste of peace and power, but at the end of the day, it was just a cop-out—I always had control, I just didn't want to take responsibility for my choices.

I had created a monster, a scapegoat that I hid under my bed, constantly fed by fear, denial, ignorance, and self-loathing. There were times when I would let it out to administer a dose of guilt and shame with a glare of disappointment in the mirror. I couldn't look it in the eye because it was the encapsulation of what I believed about myself—that I did horrible things on purpose.

The truth, however, is that education, acceptance, and forgiveness lifted the veil I had come to hide it behind. Every day, I found I had an opportunity to turn on the light and acknowledge what I had created—or run and hide in the darkness, afraid of my own power.

Another false sense of power I got from suicide was the thought that I could manipulate others to feel guilt—to think of what they should have and could have done to prevent my self-inflicted death. I had the power to force my will on them as if I knew what was best for them. In truth, I was too lazy to put in the work to help them change. How ironic is it to think that, though unable to control my own life, I could magically control someone else's by taking mine?

A friend of mine had a wife who lost her life to suicide. She left an eight-page letter with instructions on how her family members should change. It included things like how her father needed to stop drinking. Each member of her family received specific instructions on how to improve their lives.

It didn't happen.

When I took responsibility, I acknowledged, "I am that Monster." It gave me the power to destroy what doesn't work and, ultimately, the power to change. I was able to redirect that energy to do what I wanted without the influence of what others thought of me, which is an overpowering force for change in and of itself.

Isn't that what a victim fears: change?

When I have a suicidal thought now, I ask myself, "Why?" Then I answer; "I can change this."

That's true freedom.

FINDING MY OWN STRENGHT

I feel a sense of weakness when asking for help, having been military trained to be the man you go to for help. This might also be because humility (not to be confused with self-deprecation, with which I have no trouble) isn't one of my strong suits.

I always thought that I should be able to do things on my own, but maybe asking for guidance on my path to change is what takes real strength.

After taking that first step towards humility—known as asking for help—I became open to change. The next step was to discover and understand the origins of my discomfort.

I also realized I had been afraid of the power to forgive, both myself and others, because it would've dubbed my previous belief wrong. I didn't want to be wrong, but the price of being right had become unbearable, leaving me with two options: change or end it.

Through change, I found that I wasn't that monster; however, I also knew I had to take responsibility for the monstrous things I had done that created the base of a monster. Believing I already possessed all the answers I only later discovered (and continue to discover), I realize now was a recipe for disaster.

Since that early time of anger and shame, each experience, each realization, and each insight has shown me that there are other options in life. With more clarity, my beliefs evolved into an understanding that I had (and still have) something to offer. The willingness to reach out and accept help from others became stepping stones to change—to a shift in perspective.

In my mission to honor the fallen by serving the living, I saw the blatant aftermath left by those who felt they could no longer face life. It was a grim reminder that seeking an early death hurts all those left behind.

I can leave before the game is over, but it won't end until I finish it. When I hid from death in a bottle, I was already dead. Suicide may seem to end the physical and emotional pain, thereby solving the problem, but it doesn't end the pain for the living—it merely transfers it with increased trauma and collateral damage.

Death is an inevitable mistress; I will not constantly look over my shoulder for Her but instead get on with living. She will come when She pleases and I will embrace Her, for She will not be avoided.

SUICIDE FIRST AID

Some people have told me they never thought of suicide. How is that possible when it's all around us? How can we not look at one of death's many aspects when it is such a large part of the human experience? I suspect they meant they never fantasized about it for days, put their name on a bullet, got the rope, or stood on a ledge staring into the abyss until the feeling passed.

You might think suicide would afford you the freedom to try anything because, if you fail, you can always kill yourself. But it doesn't free you of anything—not if you've already stepped into the rabbit hole and can think of nothing else.

When I have a moment to reflect, I look at thoughts or things that gave me some strength or helped derail that train to the rabbit hole. I recommend you do the same.

I've thought about how I want to be remembered, what my life meant, what I stood for, what I had been afraid to do and how I could use the time I had left to correct mistakes I had made. We have no choice in leaving a legacy; every tombstone has the same dash between two dates. The only choice we have is what the dash represents.

Another thing that kept me from killing myself at the time was my anger at those I imagined wanted me dead. I would be damned before I gave them the pleasure of my death; I would be here just to piss them off and continue to make their lives miserable. Letting go of that anger, however, is what gave me true strength to continue, no more the victim.

Doing something physical when a negative thought arises is another technique I often used. Owning a gym was very helpful because the opportunity for physical exertion was always available. A Chaplain friend of mine who served during the second half of the Iraq War said he observed a significant difference in issues (suicide, PTSD, etc.) between those who returned home and engaged in physically strenuous activities (martial arts, weightlifting, yoga, etc.) and those who engaged in video games. I'm not knocking video games—but I'll always put my money on physical activities as the most helpful.

My suicide first aid was similar to trauma first aid—like how medics are trained to act in a combat situation. How can an unarmed person go in under fire to aid a wounded soldier when their lizard brain has just started screaming, "RUN!"? They are trained, with muscle memory to guide them: feel your knee on the earth, feel your heart pound, breathe, focus, and so on. It grounds them for the task at hand. Just as a medic stops the bleeding, my first step was to stop the downward spiral of negative thoughts.

Having a pre-programed physical task at that point of the lizard brain helps you work through it. The mind is programmed to fall back onto something it has done before—it doesn't have to think. Creating an opportunity to not think can short-circuit negative thoughts.

Develop your own plan and run through it so it's in place when you see yourself stepping into that hole. It helps to:

- Find a quiet place and contemplate the "what ifs" and "what would I dos?" (What would I do if I wasn't afraid to do anything? What help might I seek?)
- Consider the pros and cons. (What might happen to those around me?)
- Write a plan of what to do when those feelings come up.
- Reflect on what triggers those feelings and why.
- Create a drill or exercise so you can shift your perspective.
- Take slow, deep breaths.
- Create a mantra, or a canned phrase, to repeat to yourself as often as necessary.
- Do something physical.

One of the things I did for my own mental health was pour myself into a workout or physical labor. It worked just fine, to a degree, but it didn't address the cause of the problem. Five minutes later, someone could rub me the wrong way and I'd be off to the races.

That was getting old and I wasn't enjoying it. To stop that cycle, I would take a deep breath or two and ask myself, "what's triggering it?" I would think about the memory that surfaced with that feeling, step back and examine it as it was—not what I believed it could have been. Then I would choose to see it differently or, sometimes, make a joke out of it to strip away its power or simply laugh at myself. There is great power in humor.

In my journey through life, working to heal from the many unhealthy ways of thinking, feeling, and acting that I learned from my upbringing, I have found many helpful experiences. I continue to seek out people and opportunities that open me to other ways of being—ways that reduce my pain and confusion. Annually, I seek retreats that help me bring out the best in who I am. My journey isn't over yet, but it is a journey with hope, peace, and acceptance of who I am and what I've done.

If you're still at that point or approaching it, I encourage you to reach out and accept help. As your healing progresses, I encourage you to continue to reach out, reach in and let go of what can be released. Forgive yourself.

I may not be where you are now, but I have been where I didn't want to be and I made it through. That is part of the current mission of TheLongWalkHome.org—to walk with other Veterans as they make the transition back to civilian life. It doesn't matter if it's been a day or a decade—there is a place for everyone to help or mentor others and to receive help (often by helping others).

<hr />

We have no choice in leaving a legacy;
every tombstone has the same dash between two dates.
The only choice we have is what the dash represents.

THE TREE OF FREEDOM

Stopping at a yard sale on the route to break up my routine, I was curious to find what treasure the homeowners had discarded that I couldn't live without. Could I learn something about them through their stuff? Would I be surprised by something I'd never seen?

I inspected their clothing, games, tools, and worn furniture, without finding anything I couldn't live without, and I didn't gain any real insight as to who the homeowners were. It was more or less a relief since I didn't really want to carry any extra weight. It was just one of millions of yard sales with family items from a father, mother, and pre-teen daughter.

As I was taking one last walk around, the father came up to me with a smirk of smugness on his face and said, "The tree of freedom is watered with the blood of patriots."

Stunned and enraged, I wanted to scream, "Would you water that tree with your daughter's blood?" I trembled with anger, as the tone of his voice insinuated that he thought his family wouldn't or didn't have to pay the price for the freedom they enjoyed.

I now realize my anger was because he was the reflection of who I had been: an arrogant man who discounted others, who thought he was better, smarter, richer, more privileged and, therefore, didn't have to make a sacrifice—he wouldn't be called upon and he wouldn't he volunteer.

Maybe that man was just empathizing with me, and I had projected myself onto his screen—a mini-series of the ugly, little, conceited monster I'd believed I had been for 33 years. It was the version of me who sat on his hands saying, "So what? Who cares? It doesn't matter."

You'd think I'd be happy when somebody showed me something about my life that I could improve. It surfaces a strong emotion and, with it, an opportunity to name it and ask where it came from and why.

My old way of thinking and being is unacceptable to me now. Since the time I served, our country has been involved in numerous military operations. Men and women, whose age I once was, and who could now be my children, have been sent into harm's way. Their well-being in the military and after discharge is of paramount importance to me.

Can I do enough?

MOVE A MOUNTAIN

The embodiment of fleet of foot by the NASCAR track in Bristol, Tennessee—the mecca of man and machine in full gear—I stopped at a fast-food restaurant to use their bath-room. It wasn't open, so I considered the nearby bushes. Just as I was about to unzip, a lady opened the door and asked, "Can I help you?"

"Yes, could I use your bathroom?"

She hesitated but agreed. Going in, I asked her if she would sign the petition. She agreed to that, as well, and asked, "How do you do it barefoot?" She looked down at my feet in disbelief.

"It's not the hardest part." I went to the restroom.

When I came out, she had everyone signing my petition. "My nephew came back from Iraq and said he needed help. He attempted suicide three times. Just last year, he killed himself."

She fought back tears as I said, "This is the hardest part of my walk."

Up the road, a woman pulled up behind me, jumped out of her car with a smile, and said, "I just have to know what you are doing."

After I explained, her smile faded and she told me that she was on a call line for the church. "I can't tell you how many times I get calls from mothers," she said through tears, "asking for me to pray that their son comes home the way he left. It's never going to happen, but I pray." Before we parted, she kissed me on the cheek, tears still running down her face.

Praying with my lips is something I do when I'm too far away to work with my hands. People say that prayer moves mountains. My experience is that, when I pray to move a mountain, I find a shovel in my bed the next morning.

THE DOG

It was a hot day in August and tractor-trailers were screaming by, blowing my hat off and whipping me around as I trudged down a shortcut—a two-lane road with six-inch shoulders. A truck with a whip antenna pulled off the road and stopped in a driveway. A woman got out, wearing the makeup of constant grief, and asked in an apologetic voice, "Can I take your picture?"

I consented. After taking the picture, she said, "I have a nephew over in Afghanistan and my son-in-law just came back. He's so angry. I didn't realize how worried I was about it till I saw your sign. My daughter wouldn't tell me what was going on with her husband till she brought her dog back home."

A story about a dog—I was relieved. "It's not sleeping or eating. Its hair is falling out. It looks terrible and it's only a dog for God's sake." My relief faded. "One of his friends had just committed suicide and, since then, he has drawn a gun on his father, on himself, and on my daughter. We don't know what to do. He won't listen to anyone." She sobbed in a whisper, "My daughter is pregnant with his child."

I asked her if I could take her picture, and she consented. That was the first time I had ever taken a picture of a mother grieving. Most of the time I was too overwhelmed from feeling their pain and I thought it would be invasive, sharing their grief with the world.

If we don't start treating it differently, though, it will never change. I want you to see the face of pain and grief that I see. Go to a neighbor who has lost a child to war, look them in the eye, and tell them you're sorry for your part. Then listen.

We hope the further we are from the impact zone, the less collateral damage there is, but that's just a lie we tell ourselves. The damage colors every aspect of life. Why do we accept this as normal? Screw normal; I want to be healthy.

GARBAGE

What is normal? My most painful memory is not a physical wound you can dress, but a mental one. Words were the club that left no visible scars. There was no Band-Aid for that kind of wound.

It was a weekend morning. My father had just finished his liquid breakfast of three shots in his oversized, overstuffed armchair in the living room, where he was king and ruled with a wooden rod, so as not to spoil the child.

"Stand on that spot," he said in that authoritative voice he used when hell was coming to lunch, as he pointed to the spot to eliminate any guesswork on my part. I looked down at my feet, making sure they covered the stain on the rug, the same spot our dog Betsy sat on when he trained her. "Why didn't you empty the garbage?"

I was five years old with an attention span of seconds. Why did I do or not do anything? I said, "I don't know," which seemed like a valid answer, considering that I had none other than "because."

"You don't love me."

"I do," I said, already in a panic, but how can you believe a five-year-old that can't remember to empty the garbage?

"No, you don't. If you did, you would've done it."

I burst out bawling, trembling as my body went into adrenal shock thinking it's not true, but it must be—how I could be so bad as to not love my father? How terrible am I? I didn't even remember that I was supposed to take out the trash; I just forgot, or did I? I was crushed by the weight of my lovelessness. Through tears, I said, "I love you."

"Stop your crying or I'll give you something to cry about!"

I was sobbing with snot all over my face, doing my best to stop, not wanting the bonus of a physical beating. He said, "Come here give me a hug." I went into his arms. "It's okay."

It was okay, but I would never shake the impact of those words: "You don't love me."

I would have rather have received a beating than the feeling of shame, guilt, and lovelessness I experienced that morning. It has haunted all my relationships ever since, as I often struggled with the notion that I'm not good enough to be loved; I had to earn that gift.

For most of my life, I have tried to prove that I was capable of love. I have worked to see things in my past with different eyes—to see the truth of the situation, instead of the truth created by his words. I often struggled with accepting my interpretation of events. I learned in time, however, that by hanging onto his interpretation, I had given my power away.

I was not just a character in someone else's book. I could become the author of my own. I was allowed to change the past—not its events, but certainly the meaning I give them.

By shifting my perspective, I am able to see the effect of those words and events, and I can change how they affect me in the present.

I was not just a character in someone else's book.
I could become the author of my own.

MISSING JEWELS

As I went around a bend in a heavily wooded, sparsely populated area, a woman ran out of her house and said, "I saw you on TV. God bless you and all Vets! I wanted to take a picture of us together, but I don't have a camera."

I suggested we take the picture with my cell phone. "Your daughter can download it off of our web page when we put it up in a little while."

Her husband came out and took our picture. She was so happy and gave me a handful of change. "We live on 200 dollars a month from social security. I wish we could give you more." As we talked, I noted that her jewelry was missing stones.

After leaving them, I cried, remembering how my grandmother stitched her own clothes and made her own soap. She had jewelry like that. She had gone without many things so she could get me little gifts.

I didn't understand giving until recently. It seems I spent my whole life taking.

———◆•◆•◆———

I didn't understand giving until recently.
It seems I spent my whole life taking.

BABCIA

At the age of seven, I walked by myself through the backyards of four houses to my Babcia's (Polish for grandmother) house. I arrived to find her standing in front of the stove with her apron on, coated in flour from an apple pie she was making. She turned around with a smile that was just for me and wrapped me in a Babcia hug, which I loved, wedged between two massive breasts, squeezed so tight—just short of suffocation and broken ribs (call me a masochist). Seconds after she let me go, my father stormed up to her door and yelled, "Where is he?"

She stepped in front of me and said, "Get out of here. You don't touch him in my house." There was a moment of silence. He turned around and walked away, mumbling.

It was the first time I saw someone fearlessly stand up to him, and him back down. I'd been holding my breath the whole time and had finally started to breathe again. I knew I was loved and safe in Babcia's house.

She died two years later. Because of her and a few others in my life like her, there was a seed of doubt that I wasn't totally unlovable; there was hope.

I knew I was loved and safe in Babcia's house.

THE VA HOPITAL

I detoured from my route to be a guest speaker at the Nashville VA Hospital. It was a rare day of not pounding the pavement and it was a big deal because of the vetting process required to speak at a government facility.

An administrator in the VA who had previously heard me speak took the time to go through the detailed process of getting me approved as a speaker at the hospital. This consisted of a background check that was followed by a complementary physical examination of my feet (I was surprised they didn't insist on a mental examination).

When Valeria and I arrived, we parked in the yard of a Veteran who had heard about our cause and invited us into his home. While in his home, we talked to the group of friends he had invited to meet us. Our conversation headed south when they began voicing their feelings about the VA, finding fault in everything they did, and wanting us to yell at whoever was in charge.

At one point, a Vet from my era asked in anger, "Who are you speaking to at the VA?"

"Humans, I hope!" That ended the conversation. In my mind, I'd just shown them how silly that question was by giving them an equally silly answer. In reality, though, I was just an asshole because I didn't know how to engage in a civil disagreement or control my anger in a confrontation.

When we arrived at the hospital, I was happy to find everyone was human. They gave us a tour and showed us all the programs they had and the ones they were in the process of starting. Before letting us interact with the clientele, they said, "Please, don't say anything negative about the VA."

"It's my fault there's a problem," I said, "Please help me fix it." Knowing they would not have to defend themselves, they were at ease and able to listen.

More than 150 Veterans and staff signed our petition as we stood in the lobby sharing hugs, tears, and joy with everyone we met. We were treated like royalty and, at the end of the day, the director told us it was the most positive and well-attended event they had ever had.

SORRY TO DISSAPOINT

The next morning I was back on the job and walking to Lascassas, Tennessee, along Route 96 in a fog so thick that I could only see a few feet ahead. It was a completely different experience from the day before.

A woman pulled up, rolled down her window, and said, "I saw you earlier this morning and thought you were going to commit suicide. Why haven't you done it yet?"

"Thanks for your concern. Sorry to disappoint you. If I was going to do it, I wouldn't be carrying a sign; I would have done it already. Do you have any water? I'm dying out here."

"No, but I would be glad to get you some." I thanked her, and she did return with water.

At the beginning of my journey, I was surprised when the police would show up, saying someone called in with a warning that I was going to commit suicide.

Didn't they read the sign? If they really thought that, why didn't they do something themselves (like stop)? Were they really that busy? Was I not worth the time it would take, or were they too afraid?

Maybe most of the people who stopped cared enough because they had already lost someone to suicide and didn't want the additional guilt of not having taken the time to find out if I was next.

Thanks for your concern.
Sorry to disappoint you.

MAILING LIST

The following day, I deviated from my course to go through Murfreesboro instead of Smyrna in the hopes of more traffic and, subsequently, more signatures.

Coming upon a man in a bathrobe going to his mailbox for the Sunday paper, I asked him to sign the petition. He did so, reluctantly, and asked if he would be on a mailing list.

I told him, "No."

Ten minutes later down the road, a car pulled up behind me. It was the man who had just signed. He came up to me and said, "I want to read it. I don't sign anything without reading it." (Bear in mind, he had just read it ten minutes prior.)

"Sure," I said, handing him the clipboard.

"Okay. I don't want to be on a mailing list." He got in his car and left.

Ten minutes later, he pulled up behind me again, got out, and said, "I can't find you on the Internet. I want to take my name off."

"Did you look up thelongwalkhome.org?"

"I probably didn't put the dot org on then end."

He scribbled his name off the list.

"When you do, you can sign up on the website."

"I really hope this is legitimate." He got in his car and left.

What things have I done, out of fear of something real—or imagined?

———◆•◆•◆———

What things have I done, out of fear of
something real—or imagined?

MORAL INJURY

I approached two men in a truck that was stopped at an intersection in a very nice residential section of town. I asked them to sign the petition, which they eagerly did.

While signing, one of them said, "My son was home on leave from the Army after three months in boot camp. While he was in training, two men hung themselves and one blew his head off at the rifle range."

Do we sacrifice our young by forcing them to go against their nature right after all the stuff we've taught them about how precious life is? Who is the real enemy?

Some people call them cowards. Why would you kill yourself if you're afraid to die? Could it be the fear of living with thoughts of what you would have to do to stay alive? Or is it the self-imposed pressure of not caving into your peers?

Do we sacrifice our young by forcing them
to go against their nature?

THE VET UNDER THE BRIDGE

At the end of the day, I came upon one of America's finest: a homeless Vet, still wearing the fatigues and boots in which he was discharged in 2008. His open shirt revealed ribs under pale white flesh covered with sores and lesions from the bugs he slept with on a urine-soaked sleeping bag. We stood 50 yards away from the bridge he called home and 100 yards away from the bar that served as his dispensary and entertainment center.

"I saw you on TV," he said, "God bless You." Thanking him, I asked him to sign the petition. "Shit yea!" After I told him I was a Marine, he asked, "You been to Nam?"

"No, my orders were changed. Everyone I was supposed to go with got shot."

He turned away from me, hung his head, and cried for an instant. Then he stopped, turned to face me, and shook my hand.

"They have a VA here that can help you," I said.

"I am going. That is what they taught me in the Army—to face it head-on." I gave him some money, not worried about what he would use it for. I knew it would be whatever he would need for the day, whether it was a beer or a sandwich.

When I got picked up a few minutes later, I cried. Another human walks the streets thinking he is not good enough to be loved.

Another human walks the streets thinking
he is not good enough to be loved.

HOMECOMING

I walked on a lightly traveled scenic road to end my day in front of the home of a Marine who called himself the Unknown Veteran. He was severely disabled with PTSD, being the only man out of his company to survive while in Vietnam. He was kind enough to take us in for a few days.

The first evening, we were interviewed by a television news channel in Tennessee. Talking to the crew as they set up, we learned that the cameraman's brother-in-law had served. We also learned that the anchorwoman's father had come back from the war almost a year after the government told them he died in action (Black Hawk Down, 1993). Her mother had remarried, but they let her father stay in the shed in the backyard; he was never the same.

She spoke in a thin voice from 17 years prior, unable to keep eye contact, "He would wash and wash his food." It had affected her life forever. As we talked into the camera about the collateral damage of the families, she turned her back. For an instant, she was a little girl weeping, "My dad came to visit, but he never came home."

How far can one go from home before they can't find their way back?

"My dad came to visit, but he never came home."

CIVILIANS AND MILITARY

The differences I see between the civilian and military populations are the opportunity for greater severity of trauma afforded by war. Being placed in life-or-death situations, we have a greater propensity for moral injuries going against a core belief that killing is wrong.

It seems to me most civilians think they are so far removed from this dilemma, or they are so wrapped up in their own lives they don't give it a thought, as if they have nothing to do with it. I admit this line of reasoning could simply be my jaded view of civilians after my treatment by them back in the late 60's and early 70's coming from an emotionally charged point of view, instead of a factual place. That said, blood is on all of us by our own actions—or lack of; soldiers just get a front-row seat.

Soldiers are considered property of the government, while civilians/corporations are the government. Service members are the weapon, but civilians/corporations determine when to pull the trigger, making it easy for the nation's combatants to see themselves as victims. The great PR work done by the media lays the blame at the feet of Service members to help absolve civilians/corporations, while conveniently forgetting the former is simply acting as an instrument of the will of the latter.

Additionally, the media's stigmatization of soldiers with PTS, a condition that nearly everyone has to varying degrees, is disregarded. Unfortunately, in our society, it's looked upon as a weakness, especially if you were in the military. So, instead of dealing with it, everyone around you gets to deal with it; lucky them.

Each experience we have has an impact. I know about mine by living it; I can only understand yours by relating to it, but I will never know your experience. I don't care how many movies I see or books I read about roller coasters, it's nothing like the ride. That's from one Veteran to another; civilians even less so, despite any amount of effort (or non-effort) they may make to understand.

It's irritating when 'educated' idiots say something along the lines of, "Anyone who signs up for the military knew what they're getting into."

That's like saying when you drive a car with your family in it, and you get into an accident in which everyone is killed but you, you should be okay with it because, "you knew that accidents happen; you knew what you were getting yourself into, so get over it."

It also fails to acknowledge the moral convenience of our current all-volunteer military. I wonder if their words would be different with a mandatory service contract or draft involving them or their children (my experience on the latter leads me to believe no, but who knows).

———◆•◆•◆———

Each experience we have has an impact.

PERRY COUNTY

Days later, I spoke at the Perry County High School in Tennessee, an opportunity set up by the town supervisor who worked to keep the area alive after the major industry left, resulting in an unemployment rate of over 20%. He introduced himself when I strolled through his town and warned me that the students could be rude. They were freshmen—that phase of life during which they could be either an adult or a child at any given moment.

While I spoke, they were attentive and quiet. Some had siblings in the military and cried. I told them at the start that we wanted them to sign our petition, but forgot to allow them the opportunity when I finished speaking. As I was heading out the door, one of the students ran up to me and said, "We want to sign the petition." They all signed.

"We had a state trooper speak a few months ago," their teacher informed me. "He stopped talking and walked out before he was done because they were so disrespectful. I have never seen them so well behaved for so long."

After we left the school, we returned to the town hall to say goodbye to the people who worked there. Then Matt walked us back to our camper and said, "I want to show you something." He pulled a picture out of his wallet of three guys singing onstage.

"This was me and my friends I went into the Marines with. We all got out at the same time. We literally closed this bar down that night and John took the eight ball from the pool table and gave it to me saying, 'Put this in your back pocket so you never get behind the eight ball.' He killed himself seven days later." Matt pulled the eight ball out of his back pocket and said, "This is the first time I ever told anyone. It's why I was so adamant about helping you."

He took a marker, wrote John's name on the front of our camper, and drew a picture of the eight ball.

JOHN COUTURE

As Matt stood still for a moment of silence in front of the camper where he had just added John's name, I was teleported to the age of 16. Having just received my driver's license a few months earlier, I got a call from a friend of mine named John.

John was the person I thought they based the Fonz on—not only because he had a motorcycle, a black leather jacket, and all the girls. He was a local hero for saving a boy's life.

John had a code. His word was his bond. He didn't back down, always had you covered, and he seemed fearless. One night, when I was 13, John and I rowed through the canal so I could meet up with a girl I liked. On the way to her house, six older guys from Jersey stopped me. They were waiting for me to show up.

They wanted to know if I was alone. I told them no—that my friend was waiting for me at the canal.

"Let's go visit your friend," they said, so they could beat us both up.

When we got there, John stood up with an oar in his hand and said, "Who are your friends, Zig?"

They all stopped, realizing it was him. Then they turned around and left.

Here we were, a few years later, and he had just gotten home on leave after his first tour in Vietnam with the Army and needed a ride, which I gladly provided. While in the car, I asked, "Are you going back?"

"I'm going till I don't come back anymore." I didn't say anything because it sounded like he was going to get himself killed and I didn't know how to respond to that.

A few months later, he came home in a coma from a bullet in the head and stayed at Southampton Hospital till he died, weighing 87 pounds. I never once visited him over the course of the two weeks it took him to die. I told myself I wanted to remember him the way he had been.

As an awkward 16-year-old who carried books in front of him to hide his hard-on at school, it seemed like a real big inconvenience to go see someone in a coma. Besides, what did it matter?

Years later, I felt I should have visited him so his parents would have known his life made a difference to me. Back then, it didn't seem like a big deal, but now I cry every time I hear The Boss sing, "Born in the USA."

Maybe if John had lived, he would have just been a janitor with a hairstyle from the '60s and a pack of cigarettes rolled up in the shoulder of his t-shirt—unnoticed like so many, but still alive with a code of honor as the world went down the road to perdition.

—————————◆•◆•◆—————————

I told myself I wanted to remember
him the way he had been.

CONGRESSMAN ROE

Getting an early start to get over a bridge with no pedestrian walkway, I became a guest of the state police and was escorted out of the area to start again without fanfare. After finishing for the day, I received a call from Congressman Roe's aid, who said he would sign our petition at 7:30 in the morning at the historic Hotel Peabody in Memphis, Tennessee. This opportunity came about because a reporter who had interviewed me called him about our cause.

We spent the night at George and Bev's house. They were members of Veterans for Peace, the first organization to support us on this walk.

I intercepted Congressman Roe as he walked into The Peabody. We sat down and I presented him with the petition. He read it in its entirety and signed his name. As I watched him read, I remembered the reporter complaining that he was a lousy politician. When I asked why, he replied, "Because he reads the whole bill himself."

"Isn't that what we want—patriots? We already have enough politicians."

After the congressman finished, I said, "I am honored to meet a patriot. Every politician I have approached to sign the petition has said no, saying that it's political—or asking if I was a constituent." (I haven't yet met a Service member who fights for just one state.)

He smiled and shook his head. "That's what politicians do. Stay in touch. I'd like you to speak to the Veteran Affairs Committee."

"Isn't that what we want—patriots?
We already have enough politicians."

A FATHER'S ANGER

Making my way out of Tennessee on Route 89, heading into Otto, Arkansas, a young reporter, who looked like he was on his first job out of high school (he was so pale and skinny, it looked like his only form of exercise was playing video games in the dark), stopped me for an interview.

As photos were taken for the article, a young man with his wife and newborn stopped and yelled out the car window, "What are you doing?"

I walked up and told him what my mission was. He got out of his car and told me that he was on leave. He wanted to know why I thought new recruits should get counseling before getting out of boot camp. Before I finished explaining, he nodded his head and said, "Yeah, we have a lot of boots committing suicide before making it to the sandbox."

As I explained the second point (a mandatory civilian re-entry program prior to discharge), he said, "I don't have a problem."

"You may not, but your buddy might."

He was about to sign, to help his friends when the reporter came around from the back of the car. He had just finished talking to the man's wife, gathering their contact information to use in the article.

The young man's whole countenance changed in a split second: his eyes narrowed, he balled up his fists and he closed the gap between himself and the reporter.

"Who gave you that info?!" he yelled. "Cross it out. I don't want you to use it. I know how you newspaper people twist things around and lie. Cross it out now!"

The reporter crossed it out with trembling hands. The man screamed, "That's not good enough!" The reporter tore off the paper and pushed it towards him with both hands as if it were a shield to protect him from point-blank rage.

After grabbing the paper, the young man rushed to his wife, yelling at her as she cowered in her seat, clinging to their infant.

He came back to me, still wanting to sign, but he couldn't put the pen to paper, realizing we would have his information. After a moment, I said, "Don't sign it, and please don't be angry with your wife. She only meant well."

"I guess I was a little harsh with her."

"I understand." I shook his hand, gave him my number, and told him to call anytime he wanted.

After he got in his car and left, I turned to the reporter, still pale, sweaty, and shaking. "That's why I do this," I said, "No family should have to live in that fear. How do you think that child will grow up?"

———◆•◆•◆———

"No family should have to live in that fear."

There are many instances of anger throughout the book; this particular encounter showed me how I hurt not only myself, but those closest to me that I say I love and that my anger was like a bomb that damaged everything within its impact zone and was the impetus for Challenge 3. In the back of the book all the challenges are listed for you to take your own inward journey.

BARBARA

I flashed back to when I was a child and my sister Deb was just out of diapers, yet already a cross between Mary Poppins and Pippy Long Stocking. Trying to be helpful, she showed me techniques that she had tested during certain beatings to reduce the pain. My favorite one was tensing up her rear end, making her bottom look like two huge albino prunes.

One evening, while still living in the house my father built (referred to as "the green house," a square with a flat roof and shingle siding painted green), my mom stood between us and our dad as we clung to her skirt like embroidered ornaments. I can still feel the oak floor beneath our bare feet and the hem of Mom's linen dress in my hands. I sensed her fear as she screamed, "No, Harold!"

My father drank every day, maybe to numb the pain and memories from the war. Back then, it was the mandatory way for a man to self-medicate; you weren't a man if you didn't drink, and my father ensured there was no doubt.

This particular night, he arrived home from work drunk and was weaving back and forth—ranting about something we did or didn't do— preparing to punish us. He backed off after my mother screamed at him, realizing that he was scaring the one person he cared more about than anything else. He never hit Mom, but there were times she was afraid of what he would do. He would tell us he loved Mom more than us because he could make more of us, but there was only one Barbara.

With the situation defused, we snuck back to our rooms, quiet as ninjas, getting out of the line of fire quickly as possible, praying not to attract unwanted attention and the unknown wrath that would accompany it.

COLLATERAL DAMAGE: FAITH

Moving through Otto and Vilonia towards Conway was relatively uneventful. Only one person stopped to talk. I became oblivious to the landscape at times because the scenery, though spectacular at first sight, grew monotonous after a few days at my slow pace. Valeria picked me up after I had done my miles for the day and was hell-bent on eating at Grandpa's BBQ, a restaurant in Cabot, Arkansas. I had learned early on that it was unwise to mess with a woman on a mission—besides, she was driving—so, I agreed.

Upon arrival, we sat down to eat and told the waitress what we were doing. She signed the petition and disappeared, petition in hand, into the kitchen.

She came out with an attractive 18-year-old girl named Faith, who wanted to hear our story. After we told her what we were doing, she said, "It was so stressful on our family when Dad got home from the war that my sister committed suicide a year and a half ago. I was the one to find her hanging in the barn. I just started taking medication because I still see her every day. The VA won't help me because I wasn't in the Service." I asked her to walk with me the next day and she agreed.

The next morning, Faith and her mother met us at a local gas station. While Faith went into the store to get something to drink, her mother and I talked. Apprehensive and protective, wanting her to go and not go at the same time, her mother said she thought it might be "too much" to have Faith walk. How can you put the fears of a mother to rest when she just lost a daughter in a way she didn't think possible? We agreed that Faith should just walk a few miles with me.

When Faith came out of the store, we headed down the road. After a few moments, she started smiling and talking about her sister, remembering the good times they shared. She realized her sister was in so much pain that she couldn't see a way out and she hadn't considered the full consequences of her actions.

Slipping into melancholy as easy as one slips deeper into a tub of warm water, she said, "It's interesting that you started your journey on June 1st. That's the day my sister committed suicide."

Walking in silence, I sensed she was a frail bird that thought its fall to the ground had gone unnoticed. My hope was that, in our time together, she would see that she wasn't broken; she would gain the strength to fly again.

BUFFALO

When walking through Oklahoma, I had the pleasure of experiencing Goatheads, a type of burr that makes the ones up north look like cotton balls. Stepping on one is like stepping on a roofing nail. They are three-sided, similar to the miniature version of jacks used to cause flat tires. I gave them the respect they deserved by walking on the asphalt instead of the dirt. My soles scuffed with each step, grinding off their skin more quickly, causing my feet to bleed more.

At the same time, it seemed like I was going through a wind tunnel set at 30 mph with an occasional dash of sand to loofah off dead skin. At the time, I doubted it would ever stop and remembered a quote from my high school year book: "Hounds Law: No wind is strong enough to blow your mind," a reminder that nothing could get to me unless I let it. Still, it was quite an exfoliating experience.

Walking through this area with its harsh conditions, I had some of my fondest experiences. One was unearthing fossils that compared favorably to those displayed in the local museum.

We spent some time in Shamrock, Oklahoma, where we shared a meal with the American Legion Post Commander who invited me to see his herd of buffalo. How could I refuse? He gave me a tour of his home and headquarters—transformed railroad containers—and showed me Native American artifacts and rocks he had collected on his property, a flat and dusty part of the plains with scrubby growth.

Then came the moment I had been waiting for: time to feed the herd. Excited as a kid about to get a puppy, I stood in awe as they came to eat. The buffalo were dynamite on hooves, ballerinas on steroids, compared to lumbering cows. I asked, "Can I touch them," as they surrounded us less than an arm's length away.

"I don't think you should. If you see their tail go up, it means they feel threatened and will kill you. They can jump eight feet in the air." He continued, "I have an eight-foot fence they jump over in mating season. If they go over three times, I shoot them." I asked why, and he said, "Because nothing will stop them, and they'll run into a car and kill someone." Standing in their midst, I had a sense of unbridled freedom and raw power that the first settlers must have felt.

The next day, we visited a small museum to get a glimpse of local history. There was a large display of barbed wire called devil's rope. What an appropriate name for something used in every war and country to restrict man and beast alike from something we all had free access to at one time.

Little did our ancestors know they'd slowly choke off the very thing that brought them here: freedom. Just the day before, I had stood in a herd of buffalo that were fenced in so game hunters could shoot them for the right to say they got one. It seemed to me they had taken something powerful and free and restricted it until death—to be killed at will, keeping it alive for mere amusement, as if to prove that we are greater and in control. Are we?

Maybe the only free thing is a thought, and our only true freedom is the ability to change how we think about our life's journey.

No wind is strong enough to blow your mind.

THE COYOTE

Just before Christmas, I crossed the border into New Mexico, the 'Land of Enchantment.' It was snowing, which surprised me; I had always equated the desert and cacti with heat. The snow underfoot was refreshing, covering mother earth with a blanket, muffling the groans of traffic that crawled over her, and scrubbing intrusive sounds from the air.

A mile into New Mexico, a coyote came to keep me company. She was covered with large lumps caused by the poison farmers used to kill her kind. The cause of the coyote's condition was legal, but was it moral? A feeling of sadness enveloped me as I thought about how my lack of compassion caused others to suffer, just like that coyote.

In the remote areas of the west, more Native Americans stopped to see me than pedestrians in the congested cities I had walked through. This amazed me. They had been robbed, beaten, killed, and discriminated against, yet they continued to fight alongside us, shoulder to shoulder, for this country and were able to offer me respect as I crossed their native lands.

When I asked why, they said, "Because this is our land." That perplexed me.

Wasn't it taken from them? Maybe you can't steal something from the land that is part of it. You can move a rock, but it's always one with the earth, no matter who thinks they own it.

You can move a rock, but it's always one with the earth,
no matter who thinks they own it.

NATIVE AMERICAN CEREMONY

In New Mexico, a medicine man gave me an eagle feather and invited me to a ceremony, the purpose of which was to allow their tribe's braves to heal from the experience of war and integrate back into their society. Warriors play a major role in their culture and many become leaders.

Their culture understands that the legacy of experiencing war is transgenerational and affects everyone. Unlike our mainstream society, where we "allow" war, many Native American cultures accept war and act to mitigate its negative ripples within their communities.

The ceremony to which I was invited included a ritual using a bundle of sage bound together with twine. The medicine man asked if I wanted to be smudged, a ritual in which the sage bundle would be burned to create a smoke cloud for a cleansing and purification ceremony. I answered, "Not unless you explain it to me, so it has meaning."

"I would like to teach you so you may know our ways. Many of our young don't because they're never taught."

He went on to say the shell that held the sage symbolized Earth, the smoke of the burning sage was used to purify. He raised the smoking smudge up and down to the four corners representing north, south, east, and west, signifying there is no place in the heavens or on Earth where the Great Spirit was not present.

He fanned the smoke around my feet, signifying that I walk with the Great Spirit, around my hands, signifying that I do His work, and then around my chest's heart-center, so I would become fearless and at one with the Great Spirit. Next, he moved the smoking sage around my lips, so I would only speak His words, around my eyes, so that I would see the world as He did, and around my ears so that I would hear His words in every circumstance.

The smudging was completed when the smoking sage moved around my head to quiet my child's mind, so I would have only the Great Spirit's thoughts.

Was that the thread of truth that runs through all religions: to accept and be open to a power greater than yourself, a part of me that I had been trying to deny most of my life? I am one with all, not separate and alone.

I am one with all, not separate and alone.

NATIVE AMERICAN GRANDMOTHERS

While I climbed up a mountain road, a bus pulled up on the shoulder, overlooking a scenic view in front of me: huge red rocks, chiseled by the trauma of windblown sand dotting an endless desert. Seven senior women stepped off the bus, not one taller than five feet, each wearing a smile that the creases of time and weather couldn't hide.

Their leader said, "We were tracking you down and wanted to meet this warrior who was walking across the country."

Standing next to the group of women with heads held high and feet rooted in the land they were part of, I felt like I was at the foot of an immovable mountain connected to the center of the earth. I listened as they spoke with pride, sharing tales of their warrior husbands, the branches they served in, and the wars they'd seen.

I hugged and kissed each of them before they gave me a gift of change and climbed aboard their bus to leave. One blushed when I kissed her and said, "I haven't been kissed in years." It seemed so simple a thing, I had forgotten what power it held.

AN ENDLESS TRAIL OF TEARS

After passing through Thoreau, New Mexico, and over the Continental Divide, a Native American Marine stopped his car and said, "At first, I thought you were working for Burger King until I read the sign. Thank you. Where are you from?"

"New York, but I've been on the reservation so long that I don't like white men either."

He laughed. "So, you think Custer had it coming to him?"

"In my book, he did."

I had been walking along the Trail of Tears since Arkansas. We hugged, and he drove off after giving me his USMC tie clip.

As he rode away, I remembered going through the south not too many months prior and telling a rebel, "I've been in the south so long that I don't like Yankees either." I had passed graveyards full of Confederate soldiers next to memorials describing how badly the north beat the south. It was offensive to me, even though my ancestors weren't even in that war.

My whole walk was America's Trail of Tears, from the birth of our nation at Concord, Massachusetts to the Boston Tea Party, along Paul Revere's ride, through Ground Zero and all the wars in the Middle East that it spawned, along the retreat of the Confederacy during the Civil War, through its battlefields and finally to the original Trail of Tears.

On my trip, I was able to view how both sides of the war felt and how we're still fighting all of them—wars that become endless when nations and their people keep the wounds infected with judgment and hate.

REDEFINING WORDS

I don't know if it's a mass conspiracy (stupidity) or a diabolical plan by an evil genius to get us to not learn from history by constantly changing it to supposedly not hurt someone's feelings for something done so far in the past that nobody today was there (or that, at the time, it was the norm).

What was right for yesterday often isn't right for today, as it should be, but we should also be aware/reminded of it so it isn't repeated—not changed to make it tolerable to those who scream the loudest so we forget it happened and repeat it again.

True political correctness (the way I would like it to be) should not be a lack of tolerance for how someone expresses themselves, but a lack of tolerance for someone attacking, insulting or demeaning, or marginalizing groups of people. It should be a form of guidance to move everyone in an acceptable direction.

Just as I have learned the error of my past behavior, society has learned the error of its past terminology, assumptions, and stereotypes that disrespect or exclude specific groups of people. We don't correct History by changing how we see the past, but by not repeating it. How can we learn what to do from the past if we don't really know what was done?

We just end up doing the same thing differently. I thought I wouldn't be my father to my children, I was only in a different way. I repeated the past because I didn't realize I was doing it, I changed the method, but not the outcome. Words being my poorest form of communication, watch what I do, that's what I'm saying.

We don't correct History by changing how we see the past,
but by not repeating it.

COURAGE

I met a Marine who lived in New Mexico through a friend from Long Island. When I passed through his hometown, he took me to breakfast and confided to me, "Four years into my marriage of 24 years, my wife became a paraplegic after a skiing accident. When she was admitted to the hospital, the nurse talked to her like I wasn't even in the room, saying how 99.9% of the marriages fail because of this change and how she would have to learn how to be on her own."

He smirked, "I was trained not to leave the dead or wounded behind. She's my surrogate Marine, and she has redefine the word 'courage' for me."

"I hope I never have to find out if I have that courage."

"I hope you don't either."

There are different types of heroes: those that, in an instant, jump in harm's way to save another and those that spend their lifetime caring for another.

He's one of my heroes.

***

"... she has redefined 'courage' for me."

DIRTY

One cold night in Arizona, Valeria and I shared a meal with new friends: Dirty (his trail name) and his wife, who I met through a hiker on the Appalachian Trail. We stayed at their house for a while and took a rare day off to see the worst case of erosion in this country: the Grand Canyon.

Pictures don't do it justice. I didn't have to look up to feel how small I was, a parallel to the illusion of my insignificance.

The next day, as I renewed my quest to reach the west coast, the morning was well below zero, then warmed up to around freezing with a 10-mph wind. Just getting out of the wind felt warm. I finished the day's walk without a single interaction on the road. I couldn't blame anyone for not wanting to roll down their window in frigid weather. When I got back to Dirty's house that night, he said, "I have a friend coming over that wants to see you."

A while later, there was a knock on the camper door. I opened it to find a young man standing there with a big smile. I greeted him, and he responded, "Tyvek, don't you remember me? It's Easy!"

I was surprised. I didn't recognize him because I had never seen him smile before. We had met on the Appalachian Trail three years prior when he had just gotten out of the Marines after five deployments. It was great to see him happy. He said, "I was on the trail because, when I got home, my wife said, 'I don't know who you are. Don't come back till you bring my husband home—however long it takes and whatever you have to do—because this isn't the man I married.'" It was great to hear he finally made it home.

While writing this book, I contacted Easy and sent him the parts in which he was mentioned to get his approval. He responded right away. "Wow, I don't remember the last time I cried, but I had tears running down my face as I read this. It brought back so many emotions." He went on to say, "When I met you on the trail, I was at a really dark time in my life. I was drinking heavily anytime I came to a town to resupply, but nature saved me. It gave me a necessary distraction that turned into a love.

"I've spoken with my wife about it. Why was I able to adapt or evolve through these 'experiences' and go on to live a 'normal' life, while others, including the guys in my squad, can't overcome it and succumb to a shitty life or suicide?"

"I've come to the conclusion," he continued, "that there are two reasons. First, good or bad, I compartmentalize things. I can turn it off or turn it on. If I am done with something, I bury the memories as well as the emotions attached to those memories. Second, I'm in the position to serve others, helping them reach their potential and better themselves. Everyone goes through struggles, and I've found that helping others indirectly helps me."

———◆•◆•◆———

"Don't come back till you bring my husband home ...
because this isn't the man I married."

MOCCASINS

With the visit to Dirty's several days behind me, I had five minutes left of the day's walk to make it to my rendezvous at the camper. I spent it leaning into the wind of a blizzard with my head down to keep snow from stinging my face as I continued to push on through like a guy pushing the back end of a '57 Chevy on a date that had gone bad. I arrived at the camper to find the lines had frozen, resulting in an uncomfortable, frigid night of little sleep.

After much deliberation, I caved and bought a pair of moccasins. I wore them walking the next day only to have them get soaked by the heat of my feet melting the ice I walked over. They ended up frozen on my feet.

The following day, after wearing them for just a few hours, I took them off. I felt I had dishonored those for whom I walked by not having touched the ground for which all Veterans had shed their blood.

My feet quickly became pink as a newborn and numb as my feelings had once been.

VETERAN STUDENTS

I was on Interstate 40 in Arizona, walking through an area that, if seen in a photo, would be labeled as picturesque. Yet, it took on a different dimension as the elements simultaneously assaulted all my senses. Meanwhile, mankind raced by in sealed capsules, impervious and oblivious to the effects of the environment they sailed through.

My skin was seared by the sun, the brightness strained my eyes, my feet were embedded with burs and the dry wind whistled across my ears, sucking the moisture off my body before it could take the form of sweat. Even immersed in my surroundings, there were instances during which it would all be forgotten, as I grappled to put feelings and fleeting thoughts of events into words.

While strolling along the highway like a queen out for a jaunt, waving to her subjects, a young man startled me from behind (my Spidey-Senses had malfunctioned). His name was Gary and he said, "I'd like to talk to you."

I nodded my head, and he continued, "I met my wife in the military. We got married when we got stateside and were trying to fit in. I debated going back in to support her. While we were on vacation, though, I hit a tree skiing downhill and was knocked unconscious. When I came to, she was at my bedside in the hospital. Seeing how upset she was, I decided to remain stateside and go back to school instead of the Service because I didn't want her to go through that every day while I was overseas." He continued, "I have PTSD and, for the past two days, I've been in a ball on the floor.

"Today, she came up to me and said, 'Get up. We're going for a drive.' She wouldn't tell me where—only that she would tell me when we got there. I got in the car and, after a little while, she told me, 'I want you to meet this guy walking barefoot across the country. He's on I40, coming this way.' I started to tell her that we would never find you—you could have been 100 miles away. As I said that, there you were, waving on the side of the road. So, here I am."

We talked about going back to school and the differences between the people who look our age, yet seem to be clueless to our unique reality and who lacked our life experiences.

At the end of the day, I met his wife Rebecca, who set up a speaking engagement for us through the Veterans' group at the University of Arizona. The members support one another in the transition to school life. They can relate to each other's experiences, and many eventually become advocates.

We were told that approximately one-third of the civilians attending college successfully graduate, but only 3% of the Veterans graduate. The reason for this is that most already have obligations to a spouse, children, and/or a job in addition to going to school. They also feel isolated from students their own age because of the inability to identify with them.

That is why mentoring and support are key in helping Veterans successfully make the transition. The long walk home doesn't seem quite so long when you have someone by your side.

The long walk home doesn't seem quite so long when you have someone by your side.

THUMBLEWEED

On the way to Hackberry, Arizona, while walking through the desert outside of Kingman, two tumbleweeds bounced across the road against the wind, uninfluenced by the laws of physics, to join me. Once their curiosity was satisfied, they veered off on their own journey.

I met the local commandant of the Marine Veterans, Shelly, when he stopped his car along the side of the road to talk to me. He invited me to speak to a biker club led by a 20-year Navy SEAL Veteran.

We gathered at the small bar, which reminded me of someone's basement where we used to drink when underage. It had real wood panels and memorabilia from a time long gone. Valeria sat across from me at the only table with empty seats. On my left was a big guy about 6' 2" and 260 pounds—a former Army First Sergeant. He was, in all ways, serious as a heart attack, and he immediately started on a tirade, talking loudly with an opinionated attitude about what was wrong in America and how guys with PTSD were just "pussies."

Taking a breath to continue, he stated, "I just buried everything. People generally don't sit next to me. I understand if you want to move."

That explained why the seats were empty.

"It's a free country," I said, "Everybody's entitled to their opinion." Then I got up and spoke about why I was walking and our 3 points, in hopes they would sign the petition, which they all did by the end of the night.

When I sat back down, he gave us a C-note. Valeria went to hug him, but he said, "I don't do hugs." We talked some more and, before we left, he said, "I'll take that hug."

She embraced him and he wept—another tumbleweed on the journey through life.

CUFFED

On my first day in California, walking on I40, a state trooper drove up, got out of his patrol car, and walked slowly behind me. Without losing eye contact, hand on his holster, he said, "What are you doing?" Before I could speak, he said, "Let me see your hands. Take the sign off slowly. Do you have anything I should know about?"

"A pocketknife."

"Put it with the sign. Is there anything else I should know?"

"I am a lethal weapon," I said with a smile.

He stepped back. The whole time, his hand hadn't lost contact with his weapon. He told me, "It's against the law to walk on the interstate, but I am not going to fine or arrest you. Do you have someone that can come and get you?"

"My girlfriend. She's at the camp in Needles."

"I could bring you there, but I have to cuff you."

"That's okay. You want me to put my sign in?"

"No, I'll do it."

He had me spread eagle, making me feel like I was doing a split, and put my hands on my head while he cuffed me from behind. It was the first time I ever got cuffed—and it wasn't even to a bed. But hey, there's a first time for everything (and I'm still hopeful). When he escorted me back, I asked to use the situation as a photo op to send to my boys.

He said, "Okay, are you sure your girlfriend won't freak out on me?"

"She shouldn't, but if she does, you can cuff her too." He thanked me for understanding his position. He was doing his job and didn't know me. I said, "I am not going to waste energy fighting. Besides, somebody would get hurt and I would go to jail." After the photo op, he took back his cuffs (he wouldn't let me borrow them).

Once I was deposited back at the RV, he told us, "You have to take another route. This one is too dangerous for you."

"The smaller roads are more dangerous because of curves, smaller shoulders, and passing traffic."

He agreed and explained, "It's more dangerous for you, but I don't want anyone on the interstate to hit you and have to live with killing you." How nice of him to think of others before me.

After he wished us luck and left, we called to see about getting permission to walk Interstate 40. We were told the state of California would gladly take all our money for the privilege. It was aggravating.

What we were doing was illegal unless we paid; then all of a sudden it became legal. Guess I still wanted to believe in fairy tales, like common sense not dictated by politics or money. The next day, I almost got nailed on that "safe" side road, but thank God it wasn't on I40.

As I continued my walk, I passed through a town with a population of 23. I saw drifted sand that reminded me of the dunes back home, though they were out of place, considering there was no visible ocean.

A reporter stopped to take a picture for her paper. We talked about relationships—how we could get along fine with people, so long as we could get away from them. I'm perfect when I'm alone, but something mysterious happens when someone else enters the room.

What we were doing was illegal unless we paid;
then all of a sudden it became legal.

IRON HOG

We spent the night in the parking lot of the Iron Hog Saloon in Oro Grande, arranged by Don Standing Bear, a Veteran biker and minister. Before starting the day, I went into the restaurant to get coffee for Valeria (have to keep the troops happy). Opening the door, the first words out of the barmaid's mouth were, "You need shoes to come in here."

I paused a moment to compose myself, then said with an attitude, "Do you have coffee?" She answered yes, and I replied, "I'll be back with something on my feet." I returned with Valeria and flowered flip-flops on my feet. I told the waitress what we were doing as we waited for coffee.

She started crying and said, "My father was in Korea and, before he committed suicide, he tried to become a mercenary. They wouldn't take him. They said he was crazy. I'm sorry. I didn't know who you were. You can lose the flip-flops."

I set off for the day, thinking we should give thanks every day that all of our military personnel are trained to defend their country and protect the people in it. A rare few shift and turn on their master, seeing their country as the enemy, blaming Her for the pain of doing what they were trained to do: judge, punish, and attack. I believe that, if we didn't take to heart the immense responsibility to protect our families, there would be 18 McVey's a day on the loose instead of 18 suicides. Imagine a world with such champions; then ask yourself how you think we can get there.

I want to stress this point: a lot of people are afraid of Vets because they are all trained to kill, and some even do, but the reality is that they rarely turn on their country. Our society isn't afraid enough to do anything about it because so few do turn, so it gets swept under the carpet. Look at what fear of a single virus can do; all it takes is the right PR campaign.

I ended the day in Victorville, out of balance, thinking I had gone off track. A large young man, waiting at a bus stop across the street, cupped his hands to his mouth and yelled out, "Bullshit."

He made three mistakes: first, yelling bullshit; second, thinking I would be intimidated by his size; and third, which was almost fatal, not doing it from a moving vehicle.

Instantaneously, my temper flared from zero to rage as I lost contact with logic and stormed across four lanes of moving traffic without looking. In the few seconds it took to cross the street, I calmed down and, once I was standing in front of him, looked up into his eyes, realized he was about 18 years old.

"Excuse me," I managed with civility, "I didn't hear what you said."

He stood there, not knowing whether to pee or go blind, and finally stammered, "I have some questions."

"What?"

"Well, I read that the more times you are deployed, the less problem you have with PTSD."

"Really? What branch are you in?" He rolled his eyes and didn't answer, so I asked again.

"I'm not in," he said, "I like to read both sides."

"Go in. Then you'll know."

When I walked away, my face bled molten tears because, for an instant, he had become the focal point of all my rage. He would have taken the beating for everyone that tried to hit my sign with their car, cursed, laughed, ridiculed, discounted, and shot at me. Mostly, he would have taken the beating for my anger towards myself—for the times I spoke without consideration about something I didn't know and for my arrogance when I believed I knew something just because I had read it in a magazine.

Is a trauma more painful the first time you're hurt, or do you just get used to it over time?

It took me a long time to be able to quell my reactivity and learn to ask myself: What do I want to get out of this? Is it worth it? Why?

THE SHARP CRACK

As Valeria drove us from point A to point B, she cracked open an energy drink. I told her the sound reminded me of my father pulling the tab on a can of beer before breakfast: a sharp crack followed by a metallic tear and, on rare occasions, a mild explosion if someone had shaken it before he opened it (we could get away with it once in a while, but we were tempting fate).

Afterward, he would tell me that it was I who drove him to drink, and then he would tilt his head back to give me the full visual impact of him consuming his early morning eye-opener.

With this picture still in my mind, Valeria brought me back to the present by responding without missing a beat, "I'm amazed he ever quit."

I laughed and said quietly, with a touch of melancholy, "So am I."

EATING WORMS

When my siblings and I made some comment that our father took as a complaint, he would say, "I'm going outside to eat worms." It seemed funny at the time—to think we could make someone eat worms just by what we said or did. It also made us stop complaining because we didn't have it that bad.

Little did we know, we were being groomed for the same diet. His complaint was, "I have to take care of you" versus "I get to take care of you." This enabled him to make it our fault that he was the breadwinner that had to show up every day to care for us. It was yet another of his excuses to continue drinking his liquid worms.

Rereading this, I realize that I'm digging through my life with a pencil much like an archaeologist, uncovering the effect of this event. Not feeling worthy of love, I've accepted pity as a substitute for love. I'm going outside to eat some worms. I'm grateful to have dug this deep; every time I deal with an issue, I feel lighter and freer.

I found out who drove him to drink before I showed up: his father. I was never told about him. I met him the first time by accident when we went to visit my father's grandmother, who I had never seen before either. She was taking care of my grandfather, Adam.

We pulled up to an apartment in Brooklyn in an old Dodge pickup truck to get some stuff for my Uncle Andy, a meticulous man who packed every item in a separate box, including his screwdrivers and soap, to take up to his farm in Pennsylvania. There was an old man on the back porch smoking a cigarette. He hardly even glanced at us, like it was too much trouble to make that much effort.

I asked my father who he was, and he said with quiet contempt, "Your Grandfather." I was both surprised and tentative, due to the anger in my father's voice.

As we approached, he said, "Hey Harold. Who's the kid?"

"My son," Dad retorted. That was both the beginning and end of the conversation. He didn't even get up or acknowledge me or my brother, who was still in the truck. When we left, nothing was said about him.

Later in life, when I asked my aunts about him, they shook their heads with sour expressions. "He was bad. When your father was younger, he would do practically anything to get your grandfather's attention. He helped Adam poach and steal. When your father was 17, he got arrested for armed robbery and received a choice between four years in prison or enlisting in the Army."

The second time I saw my grandfather, he was in a casket. His Dumbo ears were tucked behind his head, and his huge red strawberry of a nose sat in the middle of his face. He had died in the bowery, stabbed for a quarter on his way back to a flophouse. My father inherited all of his possessions, which fit in a shoebox. After reading the poem he found in it (something about preferring to drink than be with hypocritical teetotalers), he burned everything except the pocket watch, which I still have today.

At his funeral, the family talked badly about him for half an hour until the director came out and said, "In 30 years, I've never heard the deceased spoken of so poorly. Surely there must be one good thing to say about this man."

After a few seconds of silence, my Uncle Andy said, "He wasn't as bad as his brother."

In unison, everybody agreed, "Ay, his brother!"

If the passage about the sins of the father visiting the children to the third and fourth generations means we inherit faults from our forefathers, then it is correct in my family, for the demons with which my father and grandfather were plagued eventually became my own. It didn't make our behavior acceptable, but it helped me understand it, and where it comes from.

I don't hate my father; the only tool he had to complete this job was a hammer, but apologizing didn't give him the right to do it again and again. There's an old Polish expression: 'You can cut a cake with a hammer, but it won't be pretty.'

I know I haven't said much, if anything, good about my father. Instead, I've stressed the effect we had on one another. He loved me the best he could with the tools he had. I'm grateful for him always being there. At least he wasn't as bad as his father. "Ay, his father!"

As I walked down the desert roads of California towards the eternal horizon, I was parallel to an endless parade of boxcars. My thinking became a train track of its own, and my life a train in the night without a whistle on an unknown route. The cars carried baggage, good and bad, to stations along the way, unloading cargo or swapping out cars as I chose.

Putting my manifest on paper shows me I've towed my father's baggage of explosive anger all this time, having simply rearranged it at different stops. I thought I wasn't like my father with my sons, only to find I was him—just in a different way. Yelling at my boys or striking things instead of them achieved the same results; they feared me just as I feared my father.

I am my father, but I can choose to act, instead of reacting, to end the cycle of mistakes.

I'm grateful to have dug this deep; every time
I deal with an issue, I feel lighter and freer.

THE ANGEL

Within 300 miles of my final destination, while getting my kicks on Route 66, traversing the parched dusty desert parallel to railroad tracks, I was feeling invincible. On that beautiful sunny day, I was having an internal dialogue about how awesome I was. *I'm almost done. I'm great. Far as I know, I'm the only man to walk barefoot across America. My feet bled every day after the first month. I'm tough*, etc.

It was all grand. Nobody disagreed with me. I was happy as a chickadee in a blizzard.

After five minutes of blowing hot air up my shorts, a woman drove up, stopped, and said, "I saw you on the news and came out because I wanted to see someone who cared," reconfirming how awesome I was. "I come from a military family and it's a shame the way they're treated." After signing the petition, she continued, "You know, I'm going to get you the best lunch you've ever had."

She headed back to a little town I just passed, as that was the closest. *I hope she doesn't think I'm a vegan. I could really go for a roast beef hero.* I didn't hold my breath, considering it was 19 miles away.

An hour later, she pulled up again and said, "Here's your lunch," handing me a small white bag, the kind from a drug store, through her car window. "God bless the road you walk on. Stay safe. Bless your petition."

I opened the bag as she turned the car around to head back from where she came. I saw a Coke, a bottle of water, a Milky Way, and a package of those orange crackers with peanut butter on them. Looking up to the sky, I shook my head, laughed, and asked, "God, this is the best lunch I ever had?"

I turned around to watch her drive away, but there was no car to be seen. I was standing in the center of an eight-mile, flat dirt circle on a road straight to the edge of the earth, totally alone with a white bag in my hand.

After wrapping my head around the situation, I cried, "God, forgive me." I had expected my angel to have wings. I wasn't anticipating an overweight woman missing a tooth in an old car, giving me junk food. After all those miles and experiences, I still thought I had done it alone. I finally began to see that God had walked with me every day.

At times, my arrogance surprises even me. It was the best lunch I ever had!

PROGRESS

After the experience with my angel, whenever someone said, "You're doing God's work," I would reply, "No, I'm joy-riding. He's doing the work." God was there every day that I looked into the eyes of a stranger that stopped to share a story of the person they lost, the love that still lingered, and their grief for a child that lost their way. Every day, I met a Veteran who carried the anger I also carried. Every day, I lived in victimhood and vengeance from my childhood, hoping everyone would get what was coming to them except me. Was there a common burden of guilt in us all?

I began to understand that, when people saw me walking and stopped to see what I was doing or to share their stories, I could show them healing. I had committed myself to a very public (and, yet, private) journey of walking 3,400 miles with a mission to call attention to an omission we had all made—an omission of care for those who had served us and the families of those who had served us.

I started my journey without knowing what the outcome would be. Through my walk, I was bringing to light something that had been hidden: suffering and guilt. I was taking responsibility by becoming part of the solution. I carried my personal baggage just as I carried the sign that said, "18 Vets a day commit suicide." I was healing myself by offering others an opportunity to right our wrongs by signing the petition.

I was committed to completing my journey and its mission, and that completion was in sight. Learning to trust, I saw that we don't have to carry our burdens alone and that, sometimes, we don't have to carry them at all.

What chance did I have of finding peace when I didn't believe there was such a thing? Now I believed there was a way for me ... and the others I met. I was a listening ear, a shoulder on which to cry, a testament to those who served, and a loud, clear voice that they did not have.

SILENTLY KILLING YOURSELF

It was interesting that each area I walked through had its own unique personality. A few miles of road often presented a world totally unrelated to what I had encountered only minutes before.

After several days of walking in southern California, where I was rejected more than anywhere else I had been, I felt I had mastered the art of invisibility in a village of the deaf. Was everyone jaded or did I miss the "Severely Impaired" sign?

It seemed like I was nothing more than an obstacle. I encountered a guy who told me he had just become an American citizen. He wouldn't sign the petition because he couldn't get a job. If he wasn't going to be taken care of, he didn't want anyone to get what he thought he was entitled to, as there wouldn't be enough for him.

Another man saw me coming, pulled out his Veteran ID card, and, looking at my sandwich sign, said, "No, we're not!" Then he slowly stumbled into the liquor store, killing himself at a speed he was more comfortable with.

I stopped in a church not far from these encounters, feeling down and out, not particularly holy. I knelt in the back and just happen to catch the afternoon sermon about forgiveness. "If you can't forgive, pray that you can."

I felt ashamed and embarrassed because, just the day before, I had been invited to speak for Crusade TV, a Baptist program near Anaheim run by Reverend Wily Drake, an energetic man about my age who heard about our cause. He said, "I like to check in on what God is doing and join him."

His church sheltered 60 homeless people, down from 250. The town was not thrilled about his guests and told him to kick them all out. He refused. It wasn't his practice to turned people away. I thought again about letting what a few people say get me down.

LOSING A SON

The night before my last strides to finish crossing America, we stayed with Joe, a father who lost his son to combat. He had met with soldiers who knew about his son's death, and one had asked him how he felt losing his son. He was unable to reply.

He had thought about it for weeks and was hoping to see that soldier the next day, when he joined me on the last day of my walk, because he finally had an answer for him. He shared it with me in a hundred subtle ways: the smile on his face when he talked about his son, how much he loved him, and how he refused to associate with anyone who didn't honor or respect what his son's sacrifice represented.

He had no guilt or unwillingness to talk about it, as opposed to those whose sons' sacrifices ended in suicide. There was no second-guessing: only honor and respect.

I find it strange that those Veterans who die from their own hands don't get the same honor and respect, though the sacrifice ends the same. Showing honor and respect isn't about their final act, but rather their choice and oath to serve their nation—a choice that always carries a risk of death, whether by external combat with an enemy, or internal combat resulting from their experiences.

I wonder, what is it people feel they're sacrificing by showing honor or respect for another who is ultimately willing to give their life for them?

THE FINAL DAY: MARCH 19, 2011

A Saturday marked the final day of my pilgrimage. Bikers, Veterans, peace activists, ministers, cameramen, and people whose loved ones had taken their own lives joined us in the walk and final steps. I felt overwhelmed—as if something was expected of me and I didn't know how to act. Aside from four other occurrences, I had walked nine and a half months alone.

First Sergeant Jessie Acosta was one of those who joined me that last day. He was an advocate for Veterans and had been discharged after being blinded by shrapnel from a mortar on his last tour of duty. He walked with his Seeing Eye dog, Charlie-boy, and his friend Rusty, a renowned USMC sniper. We talked about discrimination against the blind as we walked. It was something I had never given thought to because I can see. When I asked about his family, he said, "You don't see any of them with me." To me, that was a greater cost of defending America than losing his eyesight.

Every day, while walking, I called a lot of people. Near the end, though, there were two people I talked to daily: my sister, Deb, and a friend, Steve Walker. I originally thought I made the calls for them, but they were really for me. Valeria had isolated herself, not wanting to hear another horror story that might jeopardize her stability. I realize now that those calls kept me from drowning in the trauma encountered every day.

My presence for others may seem to have come from a place of guilt, but deep within was a spark of strength from knowing that healing myself required forgiving myself.

I didn't know it then, but that was the real mission.

When I reached the end of the Santa Monica Pier, I took off my sign, knelt down with Don Standing Bear, thanked God for keeping us safe, stripped down to my Batman underwear, and plunged into the ocean.

The bikers simply stated, "We were with you till we saw the underwear."

THE PETITION

In the ensuing months, I struggled to reach equilibrium. I called Congressman Roe's office several times to get the date on which I would travel to DC and present the petition I had carried across America; it now contained more than 10,000 signatures. His aid kept putting me off, saying she would let him know. Finally, I called his direct line and he invited me to a Veterans Health Subcommittee Meeting three days away.

Government bureaucracy reminds me of a joke about who's in charge. Once upon a time, all the body parts argued about who should be the boss. The brain said, "It should be me because I control everything." The eyes, nose, and ears each made a case because of their unique abilities to keep the body safe. The anus said, "I should be the boss." All the parts laughed so he shut down. A few days later, the brain got a headache, the eyes watered, the nose ran, and the ears rang, so the anus became the boss. Who said you have to have brains to be the boss?

Before going to the meeting, Paul Sullivan (who, at the time, had been advocating on Capitol Hill for more than ten years, representing different organizations, including Veterans for Common Sense) gave me some advice: "Meet everyone there and give them your proposal. Everyone."

I spent the first day walking through the halls of DC barefoot, meeting people, and handing out our proposal. I didn't get to speak, but I was recognized, which I was told worked out better because everything I submitted would be entered into the records. The head of the committee came to me later and said, "If I had known you were here, I would have had you speak." I guess I should have walked more.

Both the Veterans Affairs and the Department of Defense were invited but didn't show; they would determine what the military would do. It seemed futile. I wept in frustration and helplessness; politics prevented enactment of the right thing.

THE SHIFT

As a civilian, part of your job is to be the voice of America and take care of all aspects of your life. Service members are owned by America. They're told what to do, and everything is taken care of for them. It can be difficult to make the shift when getting discharged because many went into the military right out of high school, never having previously experienced total independence.

It's easy to fall into the trap of blaming the government for what is going on because, sometimes, we don't realize we have the power to change things if enough of us stand up together. I believe it often only seems we have no power because not enough of us use it to effect change.

In the military, I had surrendered my rights as a citizen and was told what to do and when. America owned me, so anything that went wrong wasn't my fault. After getting out, I had to own America, just as it had owned me, or it would never be my country. As my country took responsibility for me, I had to take responsibility for it.

My life has been a product of the choices I have made, many to see the world, not as it truly is, but rather the way I wanted to, making this moment inescapable. If I don't accept people and situations as they are, those moments will often be miserable. I have no intention to cop out by not caring, but rather to see the love from their perspective (even if it's sponsored by fear) and to remove the barriers I built against it.

While in the military, there are a few things we experience in a way civilians do not. Comradery entails being with a group that has your back and shares the same experiences. There is a certain lifestyle that involves the ability to focus on a single task with a myriad of support. It's a career that involves getting paid to play with weapons and blow stuff up, and it creates an elite minority who are well-trained and understand the meaning behind a uniform.

In the beginning, I foolishly thought people would rally behind this cause just as they did with Mothers Against Drunk Driving (MADD). I would go to Washington DC, tell them what to do, give them a piece of my mind, and get a law passed. I would be a hero, my job would be done, someone else would do the work, and I would live happily ever after. I was wrong.

In reality, there would be days the sign I wore would be as heavy as the body bags of every soldier that ever took his life. At other times, it was the invincible shield that those soldiers rallied behind to save the living.

Most people who have lost a loved one to suicide have experienced what it is like to swim in a sea of guilt, unable to find solid ground on which to take a stand. Most people that didn't directly lose someone didn't rally behind my petition because they thought it had nothing to do with them or their children. In the end, there isn't just one person or organization to blame for the deaths; trying to place blame would call for accountability of us all. Who wants that? It would mean we have to do something instead of blaming someone else.

A month after I walked the halls of Capitol Hill, I realized my tears had been for me. I had gone to tell the government what to do with no plans of doing anything myself. Once again, I was the "they" that I had rebelled against my entire life. I was the woman I met in the woods four years earlier that tried to tell me what to do while she did nothing but talk.

I came to understand that my walk and the petition wasn't so much about getting a law passed, but rather about changing people's perception through education and example. People can be manipulated with laws and money, but what happens when the money runs out or no one's around to enforce the laws? A sure sign of virtue is just behavior in the absence of law (we don't have a law to take shelter when it rains; it's just common sense).

I finally realized that I needed to continue to be a model of that "just behavior" and continue to be proactive in helping Veterans.

My life has been a product of the choices I have made,... making this moment inescapable.

A HOMELESS SHELTER

After my epiphany that I needed to be a solution—that I am America and that I am responsible for helping solve the problems I recognize in our country (and then ask for help)—I returned to the Florida Keys.

Through The Long Walk Home (TLWH), I started a homeless shelter for Veterans and their families, which I ran for two years. I planned to convert it into a gym that would be free for Vets, so they could use exercise and physical exertion (instead of alcohol or drugs) to heal from their (in)visible wounds. Having owned and managed my gym in New York for 20+ years, I had firsthand experience.

The shelter had a major learning curve for me, considering all the fundraising and organizing we had to do to keep the doors open: paying rent and utilities, managing volunteers, creating programs, collaborating with other organizations and dealing with politics, pilfering, and false accusations.

I still had more to learn. After going home one night, a man stopped by the outdoor shower I'd built and told everyone he was my friend and that I'd given him the 'OK' to use it. After he finished washing, he took a shit in the shower.

No one staying there could clean it up; they all had some incredible excuse. I was furious and wanted to find my 'friend' so I could rub his face in it. Several days later, he did it again. Nobody knew who he was. I couldn't find him. I was livid.

Scrubbing it out for the second time, I screamed to myself, "God, what are you trying to tell me?" It finally dawned on me that that was me years ago; I would've broken the shower to prove that you couldn't help me.

We each have our own road to walk. Who am I to judge yours? On your path, you may have to sleep in your own puke; you don't need my help for that.

I had to live in anger for 33 years (and clean that shower twice) to finally get it. The man never showed up again, and I never found out who he was (probably another angel).

I'd been trying to change the world by changing others, not realizing God only gave me one person to fix (and I'm having a hell of a time with him). What greater gift could I give another than to improve and change myself, rather than trying to change them for me?

The Long Walk Home isn't simply for others; it has been my walk home—from being a judgmental victim to being an empowered, accepting, and accountable individual (and yes, I'm still a work in progress). At the end of it all, I found the best helping hand at the end of my wrist.

God only gave me one person to fix
(and I'm having a hell of a time with him).

This incident showed me I could never change any relationship I had with another till I looked at my part in it and started to accept people as they were where they were, including myself. What relation-ships would you like to change, how would you do that? This is the inspiration for Challenge 8. In the back of the book all the challenges are listed for you to take your own inward journey.

BREATHWORK

We had weekly workshops at the shelter. The topics related to Post-Traumatic Stress and were open to the public. One night, the Weldon's (a couple I had never met) drove by and felt compelled to stop in. At the end of the night, they approached me and told me of a humanitarian organization they are involved with called The Art of Living.

They invited me to visit, experience the work they were doing with Veterans, and meet the founder, Sri Sri Ravishankar (a Yogi from India I had never heard of).

I was skeptical but willing to try anything as long as I understood why and how it works. They told me that our breath varies based on what's happening in our lives at the moment: joy, grief, sorrow, rage, hate, fear, etc. Then the emotion is stored in our nervous system and can be eliminated or reversed by certain types of breathing and meditation at a later date.

It seemed odd that I had given so little credence to breathing, simply because it's something I do every day, but I knew both martial artists and great athletes improve their performance with different breathing methods. I had also heard stories about what Yogis have done for thousands of years with certain types of breathing patterns: lowering heart rate, raising body temperature, and demonstrating superhuman feats of strength.

I was still a little doubtful when I went, as I'd met so many people that talk one story but live another. I was standoffish when I first saw their founder walking around the grounds, smiling like he was stoned as his head sought to find balance on his neck, always surrounded by his peeps. He was a ball at a kid's soccer game. Jim had arranged a private audience with him. He was in a zone of bliss, making us feel like his best friend—genuinely happy to see us.

Later, we discovered he was nominated for the Nobel Peace Prize for being instrumental in ending a civil war that had been raging for over 50 years by traveling alone into the jungle to meet with the guerrillas and staying with them for five days to breathe and meditate.

In addition to a program for Veterans to heal from the traumas of war, he had built hospitals, schools, and centers of service all over the world. I could hear the man when he spoke.

At the retreat, there were quite a few military officers. I felt a lingering sense of distrust, thinking they were just another form of authority ordering me around. Did they care or know what Sri was talking about? Were they making us do something they wouldn't?

When I got to know some of them, I began to understand their perspective. I learned how they felt about those under them, the burden they carried from losing the men and women in their charge, and how they dealt with the same guilt-inducing scripts that I did: I could have... I should have... Did I do the right thing? Why?

We were the same; we did the best we could with what we believed at the time—just like my commanding officer.

It seemed odd that I had given so little credence
to breathing.

REBIRTH

From 2006 until 2019, The Long Walk Home was basically one of the many small non-profits that is a one-person show. The issue was that I looked at money as a temptation and a thing people (particularly those who are greedy and looking for fault) would focus on instead of a tool. That, and felt I could do it alone. My feet have hardened over the years— one day they may catch up to my head.

When the virus hit and the stupidity that fear creates stopped everything except the essentials (thank God that there wasn't a total departure from sanity), I was unable to go out in public and engage with Veterans (or anybody for that matter). I was, however, able to stay in touch with many people through the internet even though I am technologically challenged.

One man asked how he could help and I honestly answered, "I have no idea at this time."

A true philanthropist, he originally provided funds for me to write this book, with the caveat that he trusted me to do what was best. Over the course of a few months (and partly because of the pandemic), I realized a different approach was called for, so I hired several younger folks (two generations removed from me) that could help me reach Veterans in a different way. His continued generosity enabled us to hire a team that has done more than I could have ever done alone.

I have also come to realize that, even though people are passionate about our cause, they still need to eat and take care of their families. Goodwill doesn't cut it, and paying a fair wage also provides incentive and accountability for them to show up. Their efforts help provide a stable framework and foundation from which our volunteers can work and build.

I've also found that volunteers sometimes face situations that can prevent them from being able to participate. Though well-intentioned, sometimes life has other plans.

Perhaps the biggest impact of such funding, however, is that it has provided The Long Walk Home new opportunities and made it sustainable for the future. I am grateful to know that it will outlive me, and I have been humbled to see others connect their legacy to our mission, as well, through the provision of designated estate gifts.

This experience has helped me realize—once again—that I never accomplish anything significant alone; there are many people I rely on.

One, in particular, who I feel deserves to be acknowledged, is Terri, a kindred spirit that has evolved into more. From 2007 to 2020, she put in countless volunteer hours until I was able to hire her full-time (for lower than minimum wage given the hours she continues to work).

There is no question that Terri has protected me from myself on many occasions. Perhaps the thing I appreciate most, however, is her ability to slow me down—not necessarily stopping since there are things I am simply called to do—from cutting the lines to the dock; she has an uncanny ability to first make sure the boat is at least seaworthy.

With her at my side—and a force greater than the two of us driving and doing the mechanical work—we are continuing to assemble a team that is a well-oiled machine built to last until this work is done.

This experience has helped me realize ...
I never accomplish anything significant alone.

EVERYTHING HAS AN IMPACT

Because of all the information and misinformation that I and unfortunately my children and grandchildren are constantly exposed to I'm unwittingly killing them and destroying myself. Because I didn't shelter them from the internet or at least have a discussion about it, their innocence had been stolen; at the age of 6 they had serious doubts about Santa Clause. Now because of all the fears, real or imagined I've robbed them of hope:

1. the pandemic: isolating them from social contacts driving them into depression and a distorted reality through social media where they see instances online of everyone having a great time, but them

2. the other political party: The enemy, traitors

3. Don't talk to strangers or play outside for fear of the stranger

4. going to school: You'll get shot

5. the environment: We are killing the planet and we'll die with it.

6. the economy: It's going to crash

7. Population explosion: not enough food and water.

8. Our current system where greed is rewarded; the good of one trumps the good of all.

9. Inflation

Their solution is simple; just stop it. Mine is more complex due to knowing consequences or excuses I make up because I'm afraid it will affect my lifestyle. But what quality of life will I have if they kill themselves? Is the media and government a reflection of me or I of them? What is the agenda, if any?

I think I can get a clear picture when I connect all the dots (data), but realize I will never have all the dots, maybe just enough to be dangerous. Also, I have to overcome my fear which clouds my vision. Any data used is squishy and what I mean by that is it depends on whose you use, how many people were interviewed, when, their demographics and how you want to interpret it. Any data can be manipulated to give you outcomes you desire.

A fine example is Max Jukes vs Johnathan Edwards where people throw away the main idea because of discrepancies in some of the information.

Regardless of the data, what am I going to do about it? No matter whatever the statistics, one person close to me killing themself (that's when suicide has a face and hits home, it's to esoteric if it's just numbers) is too many. What kind of world have I created that they would want to leave?

———————◆•◆•◆———————

Any data used is squishy ...

EVERYONE HAS AN IMPACT

Everyone has an impact from how they show up and how people perceive them. I had thrown away my freedom with reckless abandonment because I didn't take responsibility for anything. Who got this power I threw away and what did they do with it? ***One of the great things about giving away my power was it allowed me to be right all the time*** because it was always someone else's fault.

It also allowed me to be angry all the time for what I blamed everyone for doing to me with that power I gave them. What really sucked about it was that I was miserable and couldn't honestly take credit for anything. What impact could I have if I gave away all my power?

You don't have to be a warrior to be a Hero because each one of us is a hero to someone. That person that you stood up for, protected, heard, consoled, shared your joy, time and treasure with. The time has come to be an Intentional Hero, where we take that extra step to reach out to others besides those who we believe we are obligated to or God had given us.

———◆———

One of the great things about giving away
my power was it allowed me to
be right all the time ...

THE THROWN ROCK

Everyone looks for "The Rock" thrown in the pond (or through the window to find the note wrapped around it, that is if you're from my old neighborhood) to blame instead of the thought that created the rock and how to change it. We are all that rock, a thought put into motion whose ripples are the impact of those actions. *The cost of Freedom is taking responsibility.* I had lots of excuses for not taking responsibility, for the ripples I made; go along to get along, you can't fight city hall, everyone is doing it, you don't want to be politically incorrect. It's not my fault, I can't do anything, but the most dangerous thought of all was ignoring that I caused ripples.

We don't exercise freedom by telling others how to be free, but by doing it. How do you do that?

By being you, not being someone else that you think you should be. You are unique, there is only one of you on this planet. Be that, it is enough, it's perfect because I discovered that when I change, the world changes and when I show up as that for the person in front of me, I give them permission to be who they are.

Veterans were warriors, but now is the time for us to be leaders. We can have a huge impact on the pond because of our similar perspective. It is like throwing in a group of stones at once; they don't create ripples, they create tidal waves. Let us be intentional and take responsibility for those ripples.

True leaders take responsibility for their actions by leading from the front, showing the way; not in the rear telling someone the way that they haven't been on. Who would you follow?

NOTHING TO FORGIVE

The hardest thing that happened to me on my walks wasn't sleeping on the ground in the rain, tearing off the sole of my foot on a rock, getting giardia, feeling that inch-and-a-half piece of glass pierce my foot, suffering a month of 100-degree weather, or traversing through the blizzard in New Mexico. It was the frail, quiet mothers that held me in their arms as if I was their child, crying and repeating their mantra: "It's my fault. I should have known. He told me. I didn't believe him. I should have known. It's my fault."

I cried with them every day for the nearly ten months it took to complete my last walk, feeling the guilt, loss, shame, and despair that their eyes conveyed when words couldn't. I thought they wanted me to forgive them.

While writing this, though, I realized that I wanted them to forgive me. In rectitude, I could feel their pain for a moment and be the voice of a million mothers, whose tongues were cut out by the jagged edge of a broken heart.

It is not your fault.

There is nothing to forgive.

Is it anyone's fault?

It is not your fault.
There is nothing to forgive.
Is it anyone's fault?

IT'S NOT TOO LATE

Almost every homeless person has burnt the bridge to their family. I'm sure there is a member of your family that has burnt a bridge. Reach out to them and ask, "What did I do to cause this? Can you help me fix it?"

Finishing this book, I have this image in my head of the present me asking the 19-year-old Ron living in the woods, "What do you want me to do?" He answers, "Just be." I finally understand what it means: I must choose between the illusion of who I think I am and the reality of who I am.

After my walk across the country, I have continued to walk five times per week for an hour. On one of those walks, I had an internal conversation:

"God, I'm getting tired. I can't keep doing this."

"I know," a voice (not my own) replied, "but I can, and I want you to keep doing it."

The next day, I reluctantly began my walk. Halfway down my route, a young man stopped me and said, "I was going to kill myself today. Thank you for being here."

I keep walking.

I have walked countless miles in my life. Writing this book has simply been yet another journey, unexpected in many ways (like every other one). I now realize they aren't separate jour-neys—merely different stages of the overarching journey that is life. And my journey intersects with many others. This book merely provides snapshots of those trailheads.

Until this point, the focus has been on the past and its impact on the present. Now let's look at the present and how it can potentially impact the future.

Please take a few more steps with me—even if you think you've read this all before—just in case there is something you may learn or simply to reinforce what you already know.

If you are having thoughts of suicide, you are not alone; help is available. Please read the next chapter.

If you're tired of the collateral damage that continues to accumulate and you want to do something about it, I invite you to join us at TheLongWalkHome.org as we work to create better resources and suicide-safer communities. Leave a review of this book, sign up to become a mentor, attend a suicide prevention workshop, or partner with us through a donation to sponsor a Vet. Perhaps consider sponsoring or helping others host a workshop. Every effort, no matter the size, makes an impact.

Finally, if you know (or think you might know) someone who is having thoughts of suicide, we have provided some basic resources and steps you can take to help keep them safe for the immediate time. It's first aid, but if you can buy some time and keep them safe for now, studies indicate their chances of long-term living go up drastically. Much like first aid, the first goal is to stop the bleeding. Keep engaging resources.

If you agree there is a problem, I ask you to consider what you're gonna do about it. If you want to be a part of the solution, I invite you to join me (and a multitude of others). I don't care if the number is 18, 22, 26, or only 1 Veteran who dies each day by suicide, because that one person could be my child. I intend to keep walking until we either reach zero or God sends down a chauffeur for me (I'm hoping winged horses and Angels).

For more information on how you can help by becoming a mentor to guide others on their own journey or to see how you might support our mission, visit TheLongWalkHome.org

How can we fully address the issue of Veteran suicide except that we do it openly, honestly, and cooperatively? How can we truly have happiness as long as one of us is suffering?

Sincerely,

Ron Zaleski

YOU ARE NOT ALONE

If you are having thoughts of suicide, you are not alone. We can't know the exact number, but roughly 1 in 12 are having thoughts of suicide at any given moment. Walk down the street; you may not see it on the outside but it's there.

You are not alone.

Maybe you're like I was, and you feel a crushing guilt about those you knew but who didn't make it. Consider the words of a Chaplain I know, "We honor those who have gone before us by how we live our lives—not by how we don't." Get help in honor of them.

The good news is there are far more resources available to you than you may initially believe. I'm not one for giving advice, but I will simply ask that you consider starting small—simply try one. It doesn't matter which one—and yes, you have the courage and strength to do it.

You are worthy of help. If a resource doesn't resonate with you, go to the next until you find the one that does.

The first resource I suggest is the Veterans Crisis Line, which will connect to a trained support person in about 75 seconds. Unlike other hotlines, the VCL uses people who have a connection to the military, usually as a Veteran, themselves, or perhaps a family member or someone who understands the uniqueness of what we do (and have done).

Here's the kicker: you don't have to be having thoughts of suicide to call. They are simply there to listen and provide support. You can call to simply talk, unload, or just have a connection with another human being that wants nothing of you other than for you to be safe. I once called in a suicide prevention workshop just to see if they are legit. They are.

You can reach them here (or text 838255):

Veterans Crisis Line
1-800-273-8255, then press **1**
or simply dial **998**

SUICIDE-SAFER COMMUNITIES

The pain and indicators of suicide are meaningless unless we have the courage to respond. The Long Walk Home's mission is to provide mentorship to individuals transitioning from military to civilian life and to provide them with positive engagements that build life-sustaining skillsets.

However, the impact of suicide will never go away unless we address it head-on, like a buffalo willing to jump an eight-foot-high fence in mating season. There are a variety of suicide-prevention workshops available to those interested in helping Veterans in need. Seek one out in your area (if you can't find one, or if you want to sponsor a workshop, let us know).

In addition to our mentor program, The Long Walk Home provides direct resources, as well. Our signature program is a two-day workshop called Applied Suicide Intervention Skills Training (ASIST) by LivingWorks. ASIST is a proven method to help people who are thinking of suicide keep safe for the immediate time, and we are making it available to our Mentors, Veterans, and anyone who supports Veterans (family members, etc.).

Funded by donations to our mission, ASIST teaches skills that enable helpers to better discuss the topic of suicide, and it is one of the best evidence-based programs for creating a Suicide-safer community. More information can be found at TheLongWalkHome.org or LivingWorks.net/ASIST

That said, you don't have to wait for a workshop to help someone in need.

The impact of suicide will never go away
unless we address it head-on.

PROVIDING A SACRED SPACE

The symptoms of suicide are meaningless unless we have the courage to respond to them. Regardless if it's someone you know well or not, if you notice any change in their behavior and suspect (or are explicitly told) they have suicidal thoughts, you can do something about it.

Even if you don't see a change, say something to them so they know you care—so they know they're not alone.

Disorders thrive in isolation.

You don't have to be a therapist or have special training to acknowledge someone or listen to their story.

Having a suicide hotline available is no excuse to not smile at a stranger.

A nod can be a conversation.

You can make a difference.

You can also become a mentor—put your own oxygen mask on first, but you can help others put theirs on, as well.

Anyone can listen. Don't underestimate this action (non-action?) as a superpower. "What's on your mind?" and "Tell me more" are two of the most powerful phrases in the English language for helping someone.

The hardest part comes next: shutting your mouth long enough for them to talk through it. In our modern world, we are often so accustomed to such a barrage of notifications, beeps, and boops, that we are very uncomfortable with silence. It's a muscle we need to build. Give it a shot.

It's often messy but that doesn't matter. What matters is that two human beings are connecting. Being present with someone and showing support—even in silence—provides a sacred space. It's perhaps the greatest gift you can provide to someone having thoughts of suicide.

Military.com provides some basic information on suicide that is a good foundation. It starts by knowing some of the things to look for regarding a person who might be contemplating suicide. Some things might be obvious—perhaps there are dramatic mood changes, withdrawal from others, increased drug or alcohol use, or directly talking about death or wanting to 'end it all.'

Other invitations may not be as obvious—hopelessness, feeling there is no way out or reason to live, depression and sadness, and excessive guilt or shame. Even lack of sleep is sometimes hard to detect despite its enormous impact on one's ability to deal with stress in a positive manner.

Trust your instincts that the person may be in trouble, and ask direct questions without judgment such as, "Sometimes when people say things like what you've said, they are having thoughts of suicide—are you having thoughts of suicide?" or perhaps "Are you thinking about killing yourself?"

Most people don't want to use the word 'suicide' in the conversation, but I recommend you do just that. Why? Because it tells them that you take it seriously enough to bring up the topic and that you are comfortable with helping them. If you try to avoid it (harm yourself, do something stupid, etc.), it's usually because you are the one uncomfortable with the topic—not them.

Contrary to some myths, asking someone directly about suicide isn't going to "plant the seed" for them (if that was the case, let me know and I'll come ask if you can give me your new phone, car, or house—you'll likely say no without a second thought because, when something has value to you, someone asking if you want to get rid of it doesn't magically make it an option for you).

Regardless, don't overthink it. Even if you do the opposite of everything above and you feel you've 'totally botched it' (trust me, I know that feeling), it doesn't really matter if you're motivated by genuine concern. So just show up and care. That's all you need. Here's a quick list:

- Genuinely care for others.
- Ask directly.
- Be willing to listen.
- Don't leave the person alone.
- Don't swear to secrecy.
- Don't act shocked.
- Don't counsel the person yourself.
- Get professional help on the phone or escort them to a counselor, chaplain, or other trained caregiver.
- If they have a specific plan, disable it by removing the lethal means of the plan (or removing them from the situation).

If you or someone you know may be considering suicide, seek immediate help—dial 911, take the individual to an emergency room, or support them while they dial a crisis line. Free, confidential help is available 24/7 through the Veterans Crisis Line and National Suicide Prevention Lifeline. Even if there is no immediate crisis, trained counselors can offer guidance on how to help someone and point you (or them) to services (for mental health and substance abuse) and resources (suicide prevention coordinators). You can reach them by phone or chat here:

Veterans Crisis Line
1-800-273-8255 (or **998**), then press **1**
or text **838255**

For additional suicide prevention and mental health resources, visit the TheLongWalkHome.org look for the Resources tab for more information.

I realize many people are unable to work the hours I have for free. Some have expenses and they need to provide for themselves and their families, but that doesn't mean we abuse that privilege. Your financial support enables TLWH to be sustainable with access to phenomenal resources, mentors, and trainers, many of whom have also dedicated countless hours to have an incredible impact for good. For those of you who think this is an elaborate scam—I simply ask you to join us and find out first hand.

ACKNOWLEDEGMENT

Most books begin with an acknowledgment; I felt context was paramount.

I had judged all who walked through the door of our shelter. I told them what they needed to do without giving them permission or tools to change, forcing them to defend themselves. I would like to thank the man who shit in my shower for helping me realize that trying to help them my way was a judgment that held me back from helping them on their journey.

FOR EVERYONE ELSE

Life has taught me that I haven't done anything alone except perhaps have a thought. So I would like to thank those who didn't shit in my shower and got me to the place I am now in a more positive way in getting this book to you. I would like Valeria to be acknowledged for driving across the country as my support team/person. I am grateful for all the parents that held me as I was their own, all the volunteers who gave of their time and resources enabling us to be of service. My team that works ceaselessly to make a positive difference.

I will just mention a few names that directly contributed to the writing of this book: Terri Miller, who did initial reviews; Babs Vitale, who cried with me weekly as we edited the story-line and captured feelings; Kali Tomasheski provided polish, making sure my English teacher wouldn't roll in her grave; and Kermit Jones, Jr., for helping me with the final chapters directly related to preventing suicide, as well final publication.

10 CHALLENGES TO SERVICE

The quickest and most effective way we have used to help people make a shift in their life is to ask questions that get them to think and eventually become an example. Our life doesn't change till we do, from a place of being which is how you see the world. We do it through 10 challenges to service which ask simple, but powerful questions. They are at the end of the book. Please look at them and take them, but know that you get out of them what you put into them and they are more effectively done in a group setting enabling you to get different points of view and feedback. If you want to go deeper please submit them to us and ask for a mentor as one of the first steps in helping a Veteran.

Through our 10 Challenges to Service which is unlike physical assistance which only helps temporarily. The challenges are a life altering change because it comes from a place of being. It's easy to overlook the ripples in the pond when you're looking for the hole the rock made.

We started taking data so we could show on paper the direct impact of our efforts (the hole in the pond). What you couldn't see were the ripples. I am a ripple of my father, a "normal" WWII dysfunctional home. Plagued by drugs, alcohol, the law, violence, broken relationships and not being supported in achieving full potential. I wasn't the only ripple my father made that can still be seen today. How do you measure the damage and scars of that human bomb, how big is the radius, how long does the fallout last? *When we assist one person in altering their life, how many people in that impact zone are changed in a way that can't be measured?*

It reminds me of the old movie, "It's a Wonderful Life" when Jimmy Stuart says to God, it would be better if I never lived. I say long as you're still alive you can still change the script in how you show up on the screen.

What ripple are you making in the Pond?

Giving should feel like receiving! No matter what cause you support, if you are giving out of guilt or expectation, why bother? If you truly believe in the cause and you get a sense of well being in the work they are doing; go for it!

It's like when someone allows me into their life to walk with them on part of their journey and they thank me for what I did. No, thank you for allowing me to be Dumbo's feather (from the movie "Dumbo" where he woke up in a tree and doesn't remember how he got there and asked the crow how he got there. The crow told him he flew, Dumbo didn't believe him so the crow took out a tail feather and told him it was magic and if he held it he could fly, and with that he flew out of the tree because he believed); you did all the work and let me in to see you shine. I'm overwhelmed by being allowed to be part of these transformations. Your support allows us to reach more people, your taking our 10 challenges helps spread this work to others, join us today and make a difference.

Just in the United States over the course of 1 year (2020):

- 12.2 million thought about suicide
- 3.2 million planned suicide
- 1.2 million attempt suicide
- 45,979 completed suicided
- Children of a parents that complete suicide are 16 times more likely die by suicide
- Veteran suicide is twice the rate of civilians
- The suicide rate of Children in foster is five times that of children in a family

Every person who takes our challenges, regardless of whether or not they have attempted, is impacted by suicide and their life is altered by making a shift in their perception that changes their life and the lives of those closest to them. They are the stone thrown in the pond that creates tidal waves--not ripples--that reach the shore.

Pre-Challenge Survey

Please complete the Pre-Challenge survey here:
https://thelongwalkhome.org/presurvey

The data from this survey helps your mentor to better understand your starting point, to help us improve this program and to help get funding.

CHALLENGE 01 EXPRESSING GRATITUDE

MORNING: What are you grateful for when you wake up?

NIGHT: Before you go to bed write one thing you are grateful that you accomplished or that happened to you during the day?

Record:

☀ Morning: _____

_____

☾ Night:_____

_____

Why? To commence a shift in your perspective, starting the day with a positive thought and ending it on a positive note.

🔊 Suggestion: Put a notebook by your bed where you will see it. Every day write down one thing you are grateful for or something positive that happened during your day. Also post positive affirmations around your living space.

📝 Notes:_____

_____

_____

_____

CHALLENGE 02 CREATING GOALS

Three things (long term and short term) that you will accomplish and the date you will complete them.

Record:

☐ Goal 1: _____

☐ Goal 2:_____

☐ Goal 3:_____

Write an hourly journal of your typical day to help you see better what changes you could make in your day to reach your goals. (Use the backside of this page)

Is your daily routine supporting you in reaching your goals, how could they be modified to help?

_____

_____

_____

_____

What have you done to accomplish your goals?

_____

_____

_____

Why? If you don't have goals, then you are a ship sailing without directions. Goals are important because they give you a target to direct your daily actions towards.

◁ Suggestion: Read or listen to, "Make your Bed" by William H. McRaven.

Daily Routine

Write an hourly journal of your typical day to help you see better what changes you could make in your day to reach your goals.

Time   Activity

_____   _____

_____   _____

_____   _____

_____   _____

_____   _____

_____   _____

_____   _____

_____   _____

_____   _____

_____   _____

_____   _____

_____   _____

_____   _____

_____   _____

_____   _____

_____   _____

_____   _____

_____   _____

CHALLENGE 03   RISE ABOVE ANGER

When you find yourself getting angry or anxious, ask yourself "What is the source of my anxiety? And what am I worrying about?"

Record:

What made you anxious or angry?

_____
_____
_____

What triggered your reactions?

_____
_____

What you did to alleviate it?

_____
_____
_____

Why? To start the process of acting instead of reacting and to reduce the impact of your emotion by writing it down.

🔊 Suggestion: Read or listen to, "Don't Sweat the Small Stuff," by Richard Carlson.

📝 Notes:_____

_____
_____
_____

CHALLENGE 04   MINDFULNESS / SELF-CARE

Be still for two minutes while focusing on your breath or listen to a guided meditation or pray. Pick a time when and a place where you could do this every day.

Record:

⏱ Time:_____ 📍 Place:_____

Start a daily exercise for self-care if you don't have one already. Consider setting a goal of working your way up to 5,000 or more steps a day.

👣 Step Goal:_____

Your exercise activity for the day.

_____

_____

_____

Why? This is an opportunity to give yourself one of your greatest gifts: being present. Also, self-care and exercise are very important to our well-being, to our physical and mental health, and it grows our resilience.

📢 Suggestion: Exercise and practice meditation on a daily basis.

📝 Notes:_____

_____

_____

_____

CHALLENGE 05　　　FAMILY / FRIENDS OUTREACH

Send a handwritten letter to a friend or family member. Take note of your expectations and reflect on what that says about your relationship with that person.

If you get a response, reflect upon how the act of writing the letter affected the nature of the relationship.

Record:

The name of the friend or family member.

_____

_____

_____

_____

Why? It takes more effort and thought, it also carries more weight with the other person that you are willing to put time and effort into showing you care.

Notes:_____

_____

_____

_____

_____

_____

_____

_____

CHALLENGE 06   APOLOGIZING

Apologize to someone you hurt and may have a damaged relationship with. What you were sorry for and what you are going to do to not repeat it.

Note: This can be someone who is alive or deceased. If the person is deceased, write a letter and then burn it to let it go.

Record:

What you were sorry for and what you are going to do to not repeat it.

_____

_____

_____

_____

_____

Why? To hold yourself accountable, take responsibility, and be mindful of how your negative behavior affected another person.

Notes:_____

_____

_____

_____

_____

_____

_____

CHALLENGE 07   POSITIVE HABITS

Identify a negative habit you would like to break.
Then start a new positive habit to replace it.

Record:

A description of the old habit and the new one.

_____

_____

_____

_____

Why? To become more aware of our habits and how they define us. As a
rule of thumb, it will take you 21 days to establish the habit as a routine.

📢 Suggestion: Read or listen to "Atomic Habits" by James Clear.

📝 Notes:_____

_____

_____

_____

_____

_____

_____

_____

HEAL A RELATIONSHIP

Think of a family member or friend you may have a tense relationship with and then write them a letter: What did I do to cause this? Is there anything I can do to resolve it? Email a picture of the stamped/addressed envelope to your Mentor or let them know you have spoken with the person.

Record:

A description of the relationship and the outcome of your encounter.

_____

_____

_____

_____

_____

_____

_____

_____

_____

_____

CHALLENGE 09   BREAK YOUR COMFORT ZONE

Smile at, acknowledge, make eye contact, and take a selfie with three strangers. Take it slow when approaching someone. Say Good Morning, Hi and How Are You, to see how they respond and if they open the door for more conversation. Be careful not to force a conversation. Someone will eventually respond in a friendly manner that will open the door for you to be successful in this challenge.

Or, you can do eight hours of community service (volunteer work) at a local non-profit like a food bank, animal rescue, etc. Submit a letter from the non-profit confirming your eight hours of volunteer work.

Record:

> The first names of the three strangers you made eye contact with and something you learned about them. Email your three selfies to your Mentor.
>
> 1. _____
> 2. _____
> 3. _____

Why? To be the difference you want to see, letting someone know you care. This is a way to acknowledge our connection with the other person.

Notes:_____

_____

_____

_____

_____

_____

CHALLENGE 10   REFLECTING

This challenge is your Post Challenge survey. Please complete this survey here: https://thelongwalkhome.org/postsurvey

✎ Notes:_____

_____

_____

_____

_____

_____

_____

_____

_____

Congratulations!

Thank you for engaging with The Long Walk Home and our mission to help prevent Veteran suicide. Completing the 10 Challenges puts you at an advantage to succeed in many of the other challenges life may give you.

Don't stop now. The greatest advantage you can have is connecting with others who can support you and who sometimes may need your support.

Join us in our online community!

Like our facebook page:

https://www.facebook.com/Thelongwalkhomeinc

Please share your experience in our facebook group at:

https://www.facebook.com/groups/military2civilianlife

☞ CONSIDER PAYING IT FORWARD

Become a Mentor or make a donation today.

https://thelongwalkhome.org/

MENTORSHIP REQUIREMENTS:

1. Complete all 10 Challenges to Service & receive a certificate of achievement
2. Take the Advanced Mentor Workshop via Zoom
3. Mentor at least one person under the supervision of another mentor OR lead the squad on Zoom group
4. Send in biography & photo

LEVELS OF MENTORSHIP:

- **Initiate:** Completed all 10 Challenges to Service
- **Mentor:** Completed all 4 mentorship requirements
- **Silver Star Mentor:** Mentored 2 people online through Learn Dash OR lead a squad on Zoom group on your own.
- **Gold Star Mentor:** Attended an ASIST workshop plus any one of our Wellness workshops, such as the 4 Lenses, the 5 Love Languages, Personal Finance, Anger Management

Ron's Walk Across America
and the Appalachian Trail

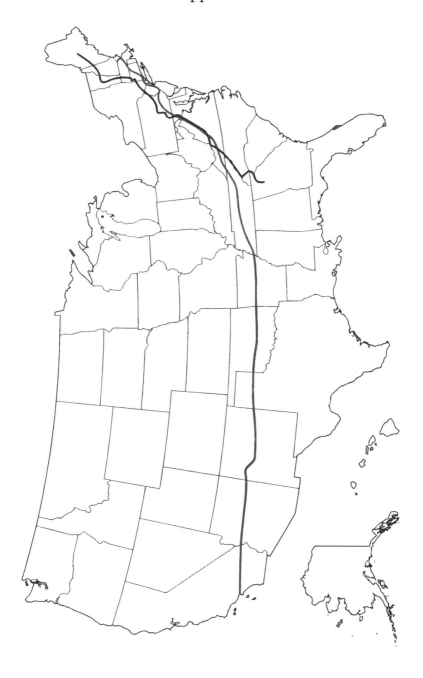

Made in the USA
Columbia, SC
02 May 2025

57477088R00140